[*See* p. 83.

A MISSIONARY IN WINTER TRAVELLING DRESS.

LIFE AND WORK

IN

NEWFOUNDLAND;

REMINISCENCES OF THIRTEEN YEARS

SPENT THERE.

BY THE
REV. JULIAN MORETON,
COLONIAL CHAPLAIN AT LABUAN.
LATE MISSIONARY AT GREENSPOND, NEWFOUNDLAND.

"Christians are some in name, and some in earnest, strong desire,
And some their Christian birthright to redeem, with cost aspire;
' A people ready for the Lord'—will not His Advent shine,
Through some courageous stewards of His grace and love divine?"
Verses for 1851.

LONDON:
RIVINGTONS, WATERLOO PLACE.
1863.

LONDON :
GILBERT AND RIVINGTON, PRINTERS,
ST. JOHN'S SQUARE.

A 2

CONTENTS.

ILLUSTRATIONS.

PREFACE.

The Author of this little Work being unable to superintend its publication, I, as his friend, undertook the task, although with great diffidence; but I soon found it a comparatively easy one. The book itself contains such a plain, unvarnished account of facts, such a humble and truthful picture of the difficulties and the encouragements of a devoted missionary, that there was nothing to be done in the way of revision, even had I felt at all competent to try my hand at such work. A few words, however, as to the Author may not be unacceptable.

The entire break-down of his own health, and the weak constitution of one of his children, determined Mr. Moreton, for a time at least, to give up missionary work in the trying climate of

Newfoundland, where he had been engaged for
upwards of thirteen years.   Shortly after his
arrival in England, he was offered duty at Romford by Archdeacon Grant, then vicar of that
place.   He joined us in our work in that parish
on Christmas Day, 1861, and remained with us
until he again left England.   Very shortly after
his taking up his residence in Romford, he was
offered by the Duke of Newcastle, at the recommendation of the Society for the Propagation of
the Gospel, the Colonial Chaplaincy in the Island
of Labuan.   This, after mature consideration,
he, to our regret, accepted.   His duty there is
to act as Chaplain to the English troops in that
colony, and to perform occasional services for the
benefit of the men employed in the coal mines at
the further end of the island.   After remaining
with us for about six months, he started with his
wife and children for Labuan in the month of
May.   Previous to his departure, he was presented by some friends at Romford, who in this
short time had learnt to respect and esteem him,
with a parting gift of some divinity books, a
handsome service of communion plate, and an

aneroid barometer. Of this last he speaks in a letter written to me while on the voyage, and posted at Singapore. He says: "You will be glad to know my pretty aneroid barometer has been very interesting and useful all the voyage. Used together with a mercurial barometer, its superiority is very evident. It has given longer warning of the gales, and sooner shown their abatement. Its reading is easier and more accurate at sea."

. Letters since received from Mr. Moreton from Labuan are full of gratitude for his safe arrival, and of hope for the success of his present work. He was received most cordially by the Governor, whose guest he was to be until he could find accommodation for himself and family, or, as he seemed to think he would have to do, until he could build himself a house.

The contents of this little book were (as will be seen by the Introduction) first delivered as an Address in several parishes in England. At Romford, I know that it made a deep, and I trust lasting impression on all the hearers. That such was the case in other parishes there is no

reason to doubt. The difficulties and hardships
of a missionary's life, so apparent, and yet so
humbly related, as compared with those of the
clergy at home, made us all think more lightly
of our own labours and difficulties. The account
of the sad deprivation of the Church's rites and
ordinances, which Mr. Moreton describes as
being so deeply felt by some of his flock, must
have made, and, I know, did make many of his
hearers feel a higher appreciation of those blessings which, from the fact of their being always
at hand, are so liable to be lightly regarded.
The faith and trust in the Providence and direct-
ing hand of God which carried him through all
difficulties, and made him take a cheerful view
of the future success of missionary labour, must
teach us all a lesson of faith and perseverance,
reminding us that we are not to be discouraged,
even though we can see no apparent fruit of our
labours.

The map and other illustrations, as well as the
MS., were begun and completed by Mr. Moreton
while at sea, and this fact would afford sufficient
apology (were it needed) for any defects in style

or delineation, the stormy latitudes south of the Cape not being conducive to the steadiness of hand generally considered necessary for the accurate performance of such designs.

In my frequent conversations with Mr. Moreton, before his sailing for Labuan, he often spoke of the comfort it had been to him, and would always be, if when abroad he could think of his brother Churchmen in England, offering up the same prayers of our beautiful liturgy at the same time, to the same God, as he and his flock were doing in a distant land. This thought he has still uppermost in his mind, as will be seen from the following passage from one of his letters: " When (please God we get safe to the end) I write to you from Labuan, I will tell you my times for service. It will always be as it has been on the voyage, of deep interest to me, to consider the times of yours in England. There will be seven hours and forty minutes' difference in our time, and judging by Mrs. McDougall's account of Sarawak, it is likely we shall be at our evening prayers, when you are at 11 A.M. service on Sunday."

I will add no further remarks of my own either upon the book or the Author, but commend it on its own merits to the regard of the reading public generally, and particularly to that of the large, and happily fast increasing class, who take a lively and practical interest in affairs of the Church abroad.

S. W. P.

Aylesford,
February 16, 1863.

INTRODUCTION.

THE narrative and observations presented in this little book are an extension of an Address delivered at St. James's, Piccadilly, at Hursley, at St. Peter's, Rochester, and on several occasions in the parish of Romford, Essex.

The kindness with which the Address was received, and the interest it excited, have suggested to me the design of putting it into writing and offering it for general perusal. I do so in the hope of supplying information concerning missionary work in an English colony, of a different character from that given in the Reports of Societies, but at the same time such as will show something of what is being effected through one of them, and what need there is of their continued and extended agency. Indeed, I will confess, it is my hope that this little book may contribute something to satisfy the reasonable requirement of those supporters of the Church's Missions whose feeling was very ably expressed in an editorial article of the "Times" newspaper more than a year ago.

Being now in no way connected with any society, further than as a contributor to the funds of one, my testimony will be accepted as independent, and, I trust, faithful; and the more so because it is prepáred and published without any notice of my intention having been given to the Society for the Propagation of the Gospel, whose work in the mission once committed to my care is here related.

Much apology should be offered for the faults of my composition. They may, I fear, be deemed the result of carelessness. These pages were begun and completed for the press amid the discomforts and interruptions of a voyage at sea. Respect for my readers, and (if I may mention it) regard for my own ease, would have required me to wait for the convenience of writing on shore, but that it seems likely that my work in

Labuan, whither I am now proceeding, will not for a long time afford me leisure for such an occupation.

If the facts here narrated are not of sufficient value to be accepted and regarded for their own sake, I can only beg to be pardoned in consideration of my purpose.

Barque "Eleanor Dixon,"
Indian Ocean, lat. 40° S., long. 69° E.
19th August, 1862.

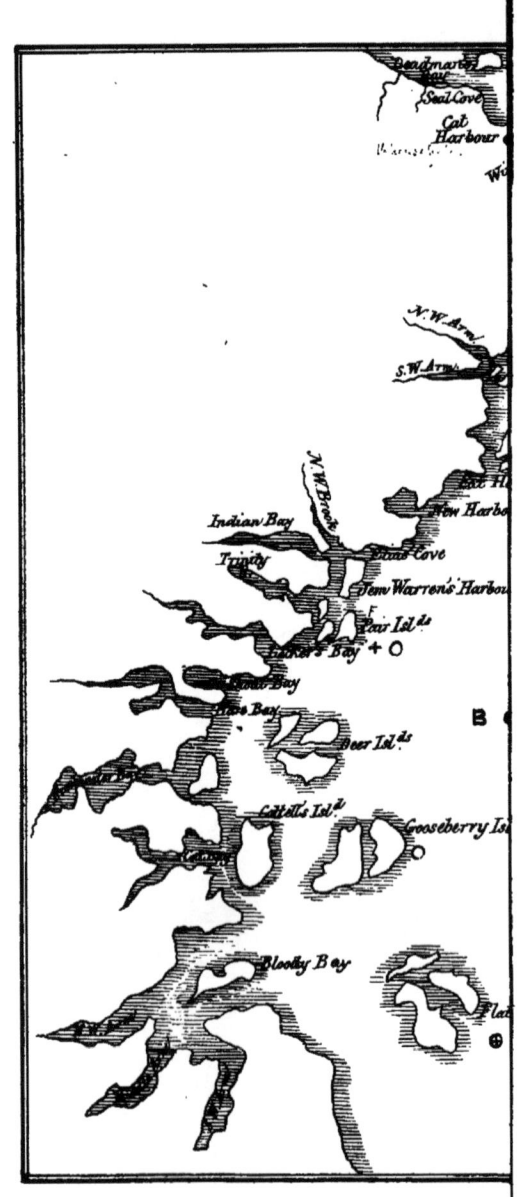

Part of the Coast of Newfo[u]

LIFE AND WORK

IN

NEWFOUNDLAND.

CHAPTER I.

NEWFOUNDLAND. ITS CLIMATE, &c.

THE extreme cold and almost perpetual fogs of Newfoundland are the most known, and to very many persons in England almost the only known, particulars respecting that country. Some reason for them both may be required, especially for the former, when it is observed that Newfoundland lies in a more southern latitude than much warmer countries in Europe. Greenspond, the chief place of my own experience and work, is nearly 125 miles south of the parallel of London, yet there a winter in which the thermometer does not descend below zero is very unusual, and in my experience it has been sometimes as low as 22°, and once, I believe, 24°. Eight degrees

B

below zero is a depth often reached. St. John's, the capital, is more than 100 miles yet further south, and still there the cold of winter is often near the same extreme.

There are concurring causes for this rigour of climate. A chief one which presents itself to my own observation, and is, perhaps, alone sufficient to account for it, is the flow of the southerly current from Baffin's Sea, along the Labrador shore, and by the coast of Newfoundland, and still southward, till augmented by another current from the Greenland shore, it meets the warm " gulf stream," which is thus diverted from its northerly tendency and turned westward, to benefit our many ways more favoured England.

I believe it is the meeting of these opposing hot and cold streams which disengages from the waters so much vapour, as to keep at least a part of Newfoundland enveloped in continual fog. It will be anticipated from this account that the southern parts of the country suffer most from the chill fog blast. In St. John's, a wind from sea does not fail to bring in volumes of vapour, which often hang for long seasons over the whole place, totally obscuring the sun and making the aspect every where gloomy, till, when the cheerful sunlight re-appears, it is matter of quite earnest congratulation. The discomfort of this foggy

gloom, depressing the spirits, and relaxing the
whole human system, can be readily imagined.
Its dangers to the mariner are almost as manifest, and need not be dwelt upon here. But it
is an error to think of the whole island as thus
mantled with vapour. In Greenspond, comparatively little inconvenience is found from it, and
one must suppose that the more remote a place
is situated from the meeting of the waters, the
freer it will be from the fog blast. Long-continued wind from the south will bring the fog to
any part of that coast in due time, but it has
seemed to me less dense, and certainly less frequent,
and less enduring, in its visits to Greenspond
than to other parts of the island. Throughout
the brief summer this cold vapour is present a
short distance off the coast, and frequently rolling
in upon the southern shores. In winter it is of
course condensed, and it comes to land in form
of snow, hail, or rain.

The heat of summer is often very great. Once
I saw the mercury rise to 136° in the sun, and at
some other times when I had not opportunity to
observe the thermometer, the heat I experienced
must have been about the same degree. When
the wind blows from the land, flaws often come
down the bays so warm as to be felt scorching
and oppressive. These are but of a few minutes'

duration. But within an hour the extreme of heat is exchanged for raw damp cold, requiring the use of a great coat out of doors, and a fire within if the wind veer in from seaward. I have been sailing in some small boat to distant parts of my mission, when the heat and glowing sunshine during the first half of the day have swelled and blistered my face, and the sultry air has impelled the fishermen who were with me to lie down on the ballast rocks or in the cuddy to sleep, leaving the care of the boat upon my hands, and almost suddenly the cold sea breeze has reached us, bringing with it the never-failing mist, and my little company at once were glad to don their heavy reefers' jackets, and be stirring in any possible way to recover their lost warmth. Under some circumstances this change proves peculiarly trying. An instance from one of my journals will suffice. Having one day been called to visit a station in my mission, comprising five nearly adjacent islands, I availed myself, as usually I did on such occasions, of the opportunity to visit most of the families there, and to hold service in their church. This was necessary, for, as will be seen hereafter, the mission being very large and scattered, my visits to each station were sadly few, and therefore every opportunity was the more precious, and to be

made the most of both by the flock and by
myself. At this time, then, on a day of great
heat, I sculled myself in a punt alone from shore
to shore of the several islands, visiting many
families while the congregation was assembling
in their church. Heated and tired I went to
the little building, and said the full Morning
Service, with several Baptisms, a Sermon, and
the Holy Communion. From the church I
crossed the water to another island to get a very
hurried dinner in a very small hot room, and in
the same room to give private Baptism to two
infants, and the Holy Communion to an infirm
person with her friends. Direct from these
duties, while feeling both fatigue and heat, I was
hurried into a small open boat to sail through the
raw south-east wind and fog, a two hours' passage
to Greenspond, experiencing a sudden change
from too great exertion to complete inaction,
and a fall of about 40° in the temperature.

Yet fine days in Newfoundland, both in summer and winter, are fine indeed, and for the
time truly healthful and exhilarating. The land
breezes of the former season are sweet with the
odours of the woods. The air then and in the
frosts of winter is dry and clear, and the skies
appear most beautifully blue. The starry heavens seen through so clear an atmosphere are

exceedingly magnificent, and very often there is
also the splendour of the aurora borealis.   Even
the fog often occasions appearances of peculiar
beauty in mock suns and solar haloes of many
combinations by day, and lunar rainbows and
haloes by night.

The severity of the winter frosts will best be
appreciated from an account of some of its effects
as I have experienced it.

All the ground freezes far below the surface,
so that when late in May I began to dig my
garden, the spade would turn up blocks of ice
at a little more than half a spade's depth.   This
freezing of the earth uplifts the shores upon
which the largest buildings rest, and thus the
floors are thrown out of the level, and often the
doors cannot be closed until they have been
hung afresh or otherwise altered.   On very cold
nights the shrinking of all the timbers in wooden
houses causes a succession of reports like the
booming of heavy guns, often continued for
several hours.   I remember well the alarm I
suffered when first I heard this in my own house.
It was very late, and I was alone, with two or
three hours' work in writing before me, which I
was anxious to finish.   Suddenly the dead silence
of my room was broken by a heavy thump, as of
a large timber thrown against the wall before

me. I got up and looked out. It was a splendid
night, the moon shone brightly above, and the
snow and ice spread every where below, making
every thing as visible as in the day.

All was still, and almost awfully quiet. In
those clear cold nights you conceive that if a
pin were dropt a hundred feet distant you must
hear it. I returned within doors and resumed
my writing, and at once the thump against the
opposite wall was repeated; then one came by
my side; two on the other side, or behind me;
a volley; silence for a time, and then again one.
I knew no cause for such sounds, and my nerves
were so shaken that I could write no more. I
went to bed, but not to sleep, for the cannonade
continued. At last, words recurred to my mind
which a neighbour had used lately, that "on
frosty nights the house would snap like guns."
It was then, I knew, a natural effect of the frost
which had thus disturbed me, and thankful for
the recollection I sank to sleep.

Often the cold renders it almost impossible to
sleep. Many such nights have I lain in more
than semi-consciousness throughout; my feet
aching; my nose positively smarting in spite, or
perhaps rather in consequence, of frequent rub-
bings. Your breath congeals in a thin casing
of ice upon your sheet and pillow, and upon any

change of your position this dabs most uncomfortably upon your cheeks. A remedy which I sometimes used, and always found effectual, was to rise from bed and run twice or thrice with bare feet upon the still colder floor. This excites circulation, and soon a glow of warmth is felt which enables you to sleep.

When writing it was necessary for me to keep my ink glass constantly upon the hob or in the fender; and the ink in my pen would freeze so as to oblige me at every second line or oftener to hold it to thaw by the fire.

No kinds of food can be kept from frost, except in cellars, which are built with earthen walls four feet in thickness. This, in a place like Greenspond where no butcher's meat could be bought in winter, was in one respect rather a convenience, for it was usual to get beef from St. John's by the latest vessel before winter, and hanging it in some store or outhouse, where it would continue nearly uniformly frozen, to cleave or saw off a joint as we wanted it. Meat and bone alike required the saw and hatchet.

The freezing of bread is as inconvenient as can be supposed, and many expedients are used to prevent it. The cellars are not suitable for this purpose because of their mouldy atmosphere. My first discovery of one very common mode of

obviating this inconvenience was unpleasant
enough. I was travelling to visit some of the
many stations of my mission, and on my way
stopped at a small island to hold divine service
in a fisherman's house, for himself and his neighbours. After the service his mother asked me
to take some tea before I went on my journey,
and I gladly agreed to do so. While cutting
bread and butter for me, my hostess complained
of the difficulty of keeping the bread thawed,
"and yet," she said, "I put the loaf in the bed,
and wrap it up close as soon as ever the boys
turn out [1]." Alas for a weak stomach! However it was *that* food or none for me then, and
I had to overcome all qualms. Little did I
suspect that in my own house any such mode
was used. One night, however, near the same
time my brother, who had lately come to me
from England, wanted supper in my absence.
The two servant girls were gone to bed, and
upon searching the pantry for himself he found
no bread. In the morning plenty was on the
breakfast table, and he asked how it was that
none was to be found the night before. The
girl's reply was, "O, sir, we always wrap up

---

[1] The "boys" in a fisherman's household are all the
males, of whatever age, except the father or master.

the bread and place it in the foot of our bed at night."

I believe it is a common practice of the fishermen's wives to keep their leaven tied in a small bag in the bed all the winter.

Another circumstance which came under my notice will also serve to illustrate the extreme severity of the cold. There was in my parlour a brick-built closet, adjoining both the parlour and kitchen fire-places, and supposed to be warmed by them. In this closet was the wine for Holy Communion. One Sunday morning I looked there to see whether the wine was put out ready for use that day, and found it then in proper condition. An hour after, when I went to take it thence to the church, it was frozen as thick as fruit jelly, and could not be poured out.

Milk freezes solid, and we commonly cut it into pieces in the jug for use at the table.

If any coffee overflow your cup, it will quickly freeze in the saucer; so that upon raising the cup to drink its saucer is lifted with it.

The door-handles, fire-irons, and all other metal that you touch cling to your hand, and will tear off the skin if you too quickly relax your hold. The grasp must be continued till some warmth is communicated from your hand to the frozen metal.

The horses at work on the roads have icicles many inches long pendent from the hair in their nostrils; and something approaching to the same inconvenience often happens very unpleasantly, and even painfully, to human travellers.

The worst effect of frost is frost-burning of the features, the limbs, or, as it sometimes happens, the whole person. The last case is fatal. Few persons that live much out of doors in Newfoundland wholly escape this evil. A few moments' exposure sometimes suffices to produce a burn of slight character; as to myself, it has happened, my hands have been burnt in the brief act of tying my cap. My ears were many times burnt. In such a case the affected part soon recovers feeling, becomes tender for a day or two, then sheds the skin, and no mark is left. A schoolmaster at one of my stations had lost great part of both hands and feet, owing to his being overtaken and outwearied in a storm. Aged people, having but languid circulation, are liable to frost-burning in their beds. A very distressing case of this kind lately came under my own observation. It is not usual for people to travel alone, from fear of this burning. The affection is attended by no sensation informing the sufferer what has happened. Your nose perhaps, or another feature, becomes suddenly

tallowy white. If you have a companion, he
tells you your misfortune, and by proper means
you restore circulation. But if no one sees the
mischief, it proceeds, and soon after you recover
warmth you will lose the affected feature by
sloughing; and though nature after long suffering will skin over the maimed member, it will
not restore the lost portion. A frost-burn seems
more difficult of healing than any other sore.
My own infant child was for many months a
sufferer in this way, though happily with no
worse consequence than a scar on her foot. A
few years ago, in the month of April, two men
and two boys went out from Greenspond in a
punt to shoot birds and seals. The drift-ice was
then floating near the shore. An offshore breeze
in the evening kept these poor men out, and
drove them away with the ice. One of the men,
who was aged, and the two boys after a time,
sank exhausted and benumbed to sleep, and in
sleep their spirits passed away, for their companion, upon their not awakening, discovered
that they were dead[2]. He kept his energy
better, and when, after (I think) three days' and
nights' exposure, he was near succumbing, he
had the good fortune to see a sleeping seal,

---

[2] This is the usual manner of death in frost.

which he managed to reach and kill. He sucked its warm blood, and was reinvigorated. For a week he remained out in horrible loneliness, keeping his punt under the lee of the ice for shelter from sea and wind. At the end of that time a vessel picked him up and carried him to St. John's. His feet were burnt, and he suffered long and severely, till a surgeon cut them both off near the instep. He still lives, and walks and works with much less inconvenience than would be supposed.

A crew of eight men, wrecked in an English vessel by meeting a strip of ice near the New-foundland coast, were brought into Greenspond in 1852 after eight days' exposure. All were burnt, and six of them had to lose limbs or parts of limbs. I was engaged in assisting the doctor in operating upon the worst sufferer, who had to lose by the knife all his fingers, one thumb, and both his legs.

Both fog and frost then, as well as many other circumstances of life in Newfoundland, are suf-ficiently disagreeable. Some things narrated hereafter may seem to those who love ease more formidable discouragements than all that has yet been told. Yet young and healthy men, fond of work and eager for adventure, will not complain

of a few years spent in such a country. Most
men know the pleasure of voluntarily enduring
hardship and braving danger, and they who in
such a spirit come to Newfoundland find positive
enjoyment for a time. Sportsmen and men of
science visit the country, and in their respective
pursuits necessarily bear rough living and face
danger, and are far from complaining of it afterwards. The minister of Christ in such a field
has, all men know, much more to impel and to
sustain him; and may hope, when he retires, to
have a far more delightful retrospect. *Too long
continuance* in hard living and heavy labour in
my own case truly made duty become toilsome,
and I may almost say life wearisome. But I
look back and remember, that at first, in fighting
against the peculiar hardships of climate, I found
delight, such as perhaps the young mariner knows
in battling with the breeze and stormy seas: in
multifarious labours I found vent for energies
and abilities (such as God granted me) which
longed to be employed: in travelling through
strange and wild scenes, and mingling at times
familiarly with people scarcely less strange and
uncultivated, my love for adventure was gratified.
And if this were all that could be said, it were
enough to forbid one's complaining of an abode

there, if its duration were not protracted too long for natural powers. I say nothing of the bliss of loving and being loved, of ministering good things and seeing them effectual, only because of this I cannot speak adequately.

CHAPTER II.

THE mission of Greenspond, to which I was appointed in October, 1849, was in most particulars the largest mission in the diocese of Newfoundland [1]. Extending along seventy miles of coast, and requiring a journey or voyage of about two hundred miles to visit all its stations in one circuit, commenced and ended at the missionary's house on Greenspond Island, it comprised twenty-three distinct places, each needing distinct visits and ministrations, and contained a population of 3700 persons, of whom more than 3200 were my own flock. A friend to whom I lately described the mission fitly named it a little diocese. It is strangely, if I may not say happily, appropriate that a charge, which so overtaxes the missionary's energies, has for its remotest station

---

[1] See the Statistics of the Diocese, published in the yearly Reports of the Society for the Propagation of the Gospel.

in one direction Bloody Bay, and at its opposite
extremity Deadman's Point. With only two or
three exceptions, each of its several stations
was a cluster of islands; and the people, all save
some half-dozen persons in its principal place,
were fishermen and their families. The fishermen prefer to live upon any barely habitable rock
near the fishing grounds[2], rather than upon more
pleasant, and in many respects more desirable
spots on the main shore. This chosen convenience for fishing involves inconvenience for
almost every other purpose. The soil, which but
in part covers these island rocks, is swampy turf.
No trees grow upon them either to adorn the
scene, to shelter the dwellings, or to supply fuel.
The gardens are potato and cabbage grounds
only. Upon many of them no water can be got
but that which drains from the swamps, coloured
like tea. In Greenspond and other places the
water from this source at times becomes scarce,
or even altogether fails. People then gather
carefully all the water which can be found in
the hollows of rocks after rain, which is named
" white water;" and when in summer an iceberg
grounds near the land, the smaller fragments
are fetched ashore to be thawed, and the water

[2] Shoal-waters.

is much valued. On these occasions a bucketful
of this arctic water was often sent to the clergyman by some poor neighbour, and it was counted
by both giver and receiver no mean gift. Once
when returning from a visit to my brother at
King's Cove, where the water was good, I brought
with me to Greenspond a two-gallon jar full, and
so much was this treat valued, that, by doling
out a measured draught to Mrs. Moreton and
myself daily, it was made to last us three weeks.
In winter, unless there is an early fall of snow to
keep the ground from frost, the supply of swamp
water is stopped, and ice or snow has to be
melted for all domestic uses.

Scarcely any one of the many inconveniences
which arise to the inhabitants of such places is
more painful, than the want of ground of sufficient extent and suitable for the burial of the
dead. An old graveyard in Greenspond, now
no longer used, had certainly sufficient depth of
swamp for the purpose, but it was upon the
water's edge, and the ice, which in winter formed
upon its banks, foundered in large masses in the
spring of every year, and carried with it into the
sea portions of the soil, till at length many
graves were wholly lost. I have seen there three
coffins open at one time, their mouldering contents being washed away by the tide. My pre-

decessor in the mission made much effort to correct, as far as possible, this sad and painful
outrage upon human feeling by procuring a new
burial ground, the best, I believe, that could be
got. But where this had depth, the graves
when dug were in a very short time nearly filled
with water. The water was baled out when at
the time of a funeral the corpse was brought to
the grave, but I have seen the coffin of an adult
person float and careen before the prayers were
ended. Where this ground was dry it was
shoal, or was bare rock only, and sods of turf
had to be brought in to build a grave above the
natural surface. Once I remember burying a
corpse, by laying it upon the rock above ground
to be thus walled in and covered. It was not
very uncommon for a dug grave to be less in
depth than the coffin.

There are yet worse evils attaching to these
ill-situated habitations. It is manifest that neither doctors, schoolmasters, nor clergymen can
be maintained in sufficient number to supply the
needs of all these places. And the labour of the
one person who in either the first or last-named
capacity has the whole care of them, is immensely
more toilsome and burdensome than the charge
of the same number of persons in one town would
be. The simultaneous calls and requirements of

widely-separated places in my mission were often
most perplexing and painful to me; so much so,
that I sometimes dreaded to go outside my house,
lest I should meet persons then in Greenspond
on some business, who would entreat me to go
forthwith, or name a time for going, a voyage to
their distant places, while my duties in other
stations were claiming my presence.

The visits of a clergyman are really and earnestly desired and valued by the poor secluded
dwellers upon these isolated places, and their
words of regret, and sometimes reproach, for the
infrequency of my visits were truly touching and
hard to be borne. No less affecting was the
gentleness and consideration of some who in
every way proved their value for my ministrations; and for such meagre services as I could
render them they were truly thankful, and cheerfully forward to serve me in return. None but
myself could well know what manifold cares and
occupations my charge imposed upon me, and one
fears it must have seemed in the sight of the
flock a scant and unloving regard which brought
me to some of my stations but thrice or twice,
or even once, in twelve months. Some places,
alas! remained even longer unvisited.

The missionary's residence is rightly fixed on
Greenspond Island, that being the largest and

principal place in his mission, and nearly central. For the purposes of trade this place is the capital of a very extended circuit. Here are two large branch houses of London and Poole merchants, to which the people of all parts of the neighbouring shore resort for supplies of every kind. Every want of the fisherman's life is here anticipated and provided for, and though some men prefer to go yearly to St. John's for their chief purchases, yet for small or casual needs they all frequently come to Greenspond. Here therefore the clergyman has opportunity for some intercourse with all his flock, and by this means he may obtain and keep a hold upon the affections even of those people whom he can seldom or never visit at their own homes. They all are glad to feel that some man careth for their souls, and receive thankfully any word of counsel and instruction. They truly value the ordinances of the Church : perhaps the very infrequency of their opportunities tends to bring out this feeling in some minds. My ministrations at the several stations away from Greenspond were almost always upon working days, yet the people did not fail to attend the services well except when they happened at some time of unusual pressure of work. The inhabitants of places which I could not visit came, often with great inconvenience to themselves, long distances by water, bringing their babes with sponsors to me for Baptism.

Greenspond is also a well-known and much used harbour of refuge, and not seldom the clergyman finds occasion for very interesting and important communication with the many strangers who, with their vessels, remain here often for days together waiting for favourable winds. Sometimes the people availed themselves of the daily prayers at the church, and some received books and tracts from me. It seemed a common feeling with them that in a strange place they might reckon upon finding the clergyman concerned for them, and ready to bid them God speed. By these means I have had the happiness of being of service to the people of some places far remote from any mission of the Church, and never, as far as I could learn, visited by any clergyman.

In Greenspond alone there are a few persons in position and education superior to the fishermen. There are the merchants' agents, the collector of the customs, the doctor, and the schoolmaster. All the people throughout the mission, except the Romanists, are English, or descendants of English settlers, mostly from Hampshire and Dorsetshire. Coming, when they were yet boys, from farm labour at home, they brought little learning with them, and some who once could read and write soon lost their knowledge. Schools supported by the local government, and by the Newfoundland School Society, give instruction to the young for a very small payment, and without payment if required; but the register of marriages, a fair test, shows that still very few persons are able to write their names compared with the number of those who, either as principals or witnesses, make their × [3].

From many causes the people generally are much altered in temper and bearing from the class in England to which they belong. They have not the benefit of living near, and depending upon, persons of higher birth, wealth, and education. The three or four persons of superior position and education in the principal settlement, are there *in consequence* of the presence of the fisherman upon the shore, and expressly for his purposes; and he well knows, for no concealment of the fact is or need be made, that they are there only for the sake of salary or fees, and would greatly prefer to live elsewhere. It is to be expected, then, that the fisherman

---

[3] Of 334 persons married in seven years previous to September, 1856, only 49 could write their names.

will be largely possessed with a feeling of his own importance. Indeed, he regards these persons as directly or indirectly maintained by himself. The clergyman too is known to be receiving a salary from the Society for the Propagation of the Gospel for his living among and serving them, and it is not to be wondered at, if unrefined minds do not conceive, or cannot appreciate a higher motive for his doing so. It is very generally thought of him that he would never leave England to dwell among them if it were not "worth his while," i. e. if the situation did not confer some worldly gain to attract him. Protesting against this notion is of very little avail in correcting it, and the clergyman acts unwisely in appearing too much concerned about it. It is part of his cross, and so to be borne patiently. One might think that the fact of the smallness of his salary from the Society *, being well known, would be sufficient to exclude this mean thought; but experience has proved the contrary. A further mischievous conceit of this matter is still prevalent with many of the people in spite of much effort that has been made to remove it: namely, that the Society is but a branch of the national government, and its funds

---

* £100 per annum.

derived from the taxes. Hence some men of my flock have plainly told me that they indirectly maintained the clergyman, though they were never contributors to his yearly collection of dues. These causes will account for the clergyman's position also being very different from that held by his brethren in England.

, The fisherman's business engaging him in much bargaining and large money transactions, is a sore trial for his honesty, and even when that stands the proof, a hard and greedy spirit, the "love of money," an *unlovely* and unloving temper, is the too sure consequence. Men who in England would be receiving daily, or at most weekly, wages of only too easy calculation, are in Newfoundland at one time taking upon credit from a merchant a whole summer's or winter's supplies at once; at another time arranging with him the terms upon which he receives from them the whole produce of that season's labour. It can easily be supposed how much room there is here for the practice of low cunning and petty scheming, and what an influence this has upon the poor people's general character [5].

[5] The scheming and cunning is commonly very translucent and easy of defeat. Apart from the solemn thought of the man's responsibility, there is something amusing in the cool impudence with which a defeated rogue bears his

Having complete command of their time, these people are of a strange imperturbable habit. Unaccustomed to move at other men's bidding, they are hardly to be excited to action unless impelled by their own perception of need. "When I see my own time," is a phrase continually in their mouths. Their very look betrays this feeling; and unless when for the moment they are eager after some advantage, their gait and every action seems possessed with a dignity, which would be ludicrous if it were not the token of so hurtful a temper. This is a chief obstacle to the missionary's work amongst them. Nothing is more painfully imprinted in

discomfiture. Submitting with the air of an injured and oppressed man to the correction of his dealings, he will exclaim, " O well, let it be so; of course it's any thing to keep the poor man down:" or, as I have heard such a man say, using a proverb current in the country, "Ah, I see it's always the same; the big fish eat the little ones." The ill-temper of such men vents itself also in low-minded speeches, contemning all knowledge of books. A man asked whether he could read and write, replied, "No, I'm thankful to say I can't, else I should be as big a rogue as those who can." Another man, witness to a marriage, whom I asked to sign the register, replied, "No, I can't write, I must trust to others, like most poor men. But I suppose there will always be some well taught enough to live by their neighbours, and do nothing for their bread." Happily most men of my flock did not think with these.

my remembrance than the long-continued effort
it cost me to surmount this, before the accom-
plishment of any work for their good.

Closely allied with this, indeed another indi-
cation of the same tone of mind, is a studied
independent bearing, which appears upon almost
all occasions. A poor man whom you hire for
high wages will say when you engage him, that
he will do the work " to oblige you."

Free and intrusive manners are very general
and very unpleasant, but are seldom meant to be
offensive. Men will enter your house unasked
to light their pipes at your kitchen fire, and
perhaps sit down to smoke and spit. Once Mrs.
Moreton was surprised by a man thus entering
her parlour, where she was sitting alone. He
said no word, but coolly lit his pipe at the fire,
and walked out again smoking it [6]. This degree

---

[6] An amusing instance of such American freedom happened
to a friend of mine in St. John's. The intruder was, however,
I believe, not a Newfoundlander, but a born Yankee. A
tradesman sent a note of some goods he was intending to
purchase. The man who bore the note entered my friend's
house by the front door, which was on the latch, proceeded
up stairs without meeting any one, went into a bed-room,
and then judging he was in the wrong part of the house
returned down the stairs. He next entered a parlour, and
passed through that into the breakfast-room where my
friend and his wife were sitting. Without taking off his
cap or seeming to think he had done any thing unusual, he
handed the note to my astonished friend, and departed.

of boldness, however, is not usual, and the persons mostly guilty of it were not members of my flock, but strangers in the harbour.

I have now named some of the most prominent faults developed by circumstances in the character of these quondam Dorsetshire and Hampshire labourers. I have dwelt upon them very unwillingly, and only for the purpose of showing with what manner of people the missionary has to work. Let me turn to subjects freer from painful thought.

CHAPTER III.

IT may be interesting to many readers to note some words and phrases commonly used by my people, which are either obsolete in England or of Newfoundland origin. Some pure Saxon words will be found in my list, and some easily traceable corruptions or misapplications; but for others it would be hard to account. I have placed the meaning after each word, with sometimes a further illustration of its use.

Ballicadoes. Barricades. The banks of ice which form upon all water-washed rocks and shores in winter.

Accommodation. Recommendation. A person of any bad repute is said to have a bad accommodation.

Gulch. A mountain gorge, or ravine; also any small fissure or crevice among rocks.

Dwigh. A short shower or storm, whether of rain, hail, or snow.

Spell. A time of continuance at labour, or a time of rest. Short distances are in common speech measured by spells: thus, "two shoulder spells" is the distance a man would ordinarily carry a burden on his shoulders, resting once in the midst.

Turn. A burden. As much as a man will carry at one time.

Charm. Pronounced *cherm*. A chant or song.

Pinbone. The hip-bone.

Kechhorn. The swallow. Eve's apple.

Soil. A mispronunciation of seal.

Ructions. An insurrection. Any popular disturbance.

Reerah. Any uproarious noise.

Illumination. A display of flags.

Ram. A male cat. The male sheep is called a buck. A person speaking to me of her cat, regretted that she could keep none of her kittens, "because Uncle Joe's ram always eats them." As sheep were kept there, I understood the kitten-eater to be one of them, and felt due disgust for ram-mutton, especially of Uncle Joe's rearing.

Human cry. Hue and cry.

Cause. Used for consequence, and vice versâ.

A person lamenting some adverse state of things will say, "I don't know what will be the cause of it," i. e. what will come of it.

Rock. Any stone of whatever size. The boyish trick of throwing stones, is called "shying rocks." A friend of mine found his servant with spectacles on, closely searching through some currants, which he was preparing for a pudding, to get out the minute pebbles found among them, and complaining loudly that he had been "best part of an hour picking out the *rocks*."

More. A root.

Tucken-mores. Small low-grown shrubs and creeping plants. I beg to offer a conjecture of this word's proper spelling and original use. I suppose it to be "tugging-more;" so named as capable of being cleared off the land by pulling up, or tugging with the hand; while the larger mores of trees have to be got out by digging and much labour.

Obedience. Obeisance. Children are enjoined to "make their obedience," which they do by making a bow.

Crabbed. Precociously knowing.

Horrid. Wonderful, but not necessarily horrid in the usual acceptation. A man, after whose "crabbed" little girl I was inquiring,

replied to my question, whether the child
grew fast, "Grows, sir! Oh, she grows
horrid."

Suant. Well continued, without irregularities
Spoken of any work or building in which the
lines are true and unbroken.

Airsome. Cold, fresh and bracing.

Clever. Large, stout. A "clever man" is a
large strong man. So a baby, a house, a
boat, a cow, any thing animate or inanimate
is called clever.

Roach. Coarse. Of large gross growth. Spoken
of timber, it seems generally to be meant
in disparagement, signifying that it is too
free and open grained to be long serviceable:
a stunted growth producing harder wood. To
whatever it is applied, coarseness of quality is
usually intended.

Brough, or brow. Apt to break, as rotten
timber.

Breakle, breakly, brockly. Brittle.

Slatterty-sling. Perhaps meaning slatternly sling.
An expressive nautical substitute for the English "sixes and sevens," or "hither and
thither."

Idle. Full of mischievous tricks. It never is
used as meaning simply without occupation.

Droll. Odd, unusual. The idea of humour is

not attached to the word. A sick person describing his feelings will say, "I seems terrible droll." When trying to show a servant some proper method of doing work, she will tell you she is "not used to them droll ways." One of these people, if brought to London, would say it seemed "a shocking droll place."

Terrible, shocking. Words used as superlatives, as, "a shocking fine day," "a terrible kind man." A man whom I did not happen to meet for a long time after my taking the mission, came one night to a house where I was staying, on purpose to see the new parson. He was noted for much talk, and what is commonly called "spinning yarns." I sat with him till his talking tired me, and I asked to go to bed. When I had gone to my room I heard him tell the people of the house, " Well, the parson's a shocking man to talk, it's no use." The last phrase meaning, " it can't be denied."

Loggy. Saturated and heavy with moisture. Often applied in reproachful metaphor to a dull slow person.

Stunned. Dull of apprehension, stupid.

Randévoo. Rendezvous. Any house which is ill regulated, and open to disorderly visitors, is called a Randevoo-house.

D

Moral. Model. As the model upon which a ship is built.

Ichuly. Puling, weakly.

Duckish. Dusky.

Sumple. Supple.

Anighst. Nigh.

Dangerous. In danger. When a sick person seems past recovery, he is said to be dangerous; which does not at all mean that his sickness is dangerous to his attendants.

Binnicky. Peevish.

Froppish. Fretful. Usually spoken of babes when they are troublesome.

Bibbering. Sobbing, and making noise with the lips in crying.

Snackering. Chattering with the teeth.

Venomous. Vehement. To go eagerly and determinedly to work is to be venomous. So also when wind blows strongly, and seems likely to last and increase, it is said to "blow venomous."

Bloodthirsty. Hot-tempered. Persons will confess themselves bloodthirsty, who would shrink from thoughts of malice and revenge.

Schram'd. Cramped, and clammy cold.

Fraw, hard a fraw. Frozen, hard frozen.

Livier. An inhabitant or liver. One who lives in any place. It is said of any uninhabited place that there are no *liviers* in it.

Nish. Tender, delicate.

Leary. Sinking with hunger and exhaustion. The feeling of a traveller who needs refreshment.

Proper. Used adverbially, in the sense of really, truly. A very estimable old person, who used to receive and lodge me in her house very kindly when I was travelling in her neighbourhood, came to Greenspond soon after my marriage. After attending Evening Prayer she waited at the door of the church for my coming out. Mrs. Moreton was the last of the congregation to leave the church, and upon her coming to the door my good friend who was about to address her seemed suddenly taken aback, and exclaimed, to my wife's great amusement, "Well, the parson have got a jolly wife to be sure! You'm a proper jolly woman, you be."

Yary. Wary.

Numerous. Filled with a large number; as "the room is numerous with people;" "the pantry is numerous with flies."

Number. Much. "I have suffered a number," i. e. I have suffered much (pain).

To Ray. To array. To ray a child is the common phrase for to dress it.

To Resolve. To answer. "I cannot resolve you," i. e. I cannot tell you.

Behave, behave your works, knock off your works, what works! Addressed to noisy children.

To Chastise. To rebuke, to admonish. It never means to punish.

Show. (Imperative) Give.

The Woman. The usual term for a wife, applied with no disrespectful intention. It certainly sounded displeasing, but was kindly meant, when I was asked by most people, "How d'ye do, sir? How's the woman?" In like manner, it was not unfrequently asked of Mrs. Moreton, "Is your man at home?" or, "How's your master?" or, "the master."

To Heft. To try the weight of any thing.

To Quat. To squat, crush.

To Stud. To think or meditate. "I can't tell, and I can't think, and I can't stud whatever I've done with it."

To Bream; pronounced brim. A nautical term of correct use. To bream a boat is to broom or brush its bottom.

Th is mostly changed to t, or d; and f to v. In foggy weather it is said to be "tick o' vog."

"T'vog is dat tick dat you may cut it wid a knife."

*S, terminal after a consonant, is changed to a syllable es; as askés, ghostés, priestés, hand-wristés. Frequently t before s is dropped, as topmases, for topmasts.

Sp, terminal, or in the midst of a word, is always transposed. Clasp becomes claps; hasp, haps; aspen, apsey; crisp, cripsey; and so in similar words. Curds are cruds, and curdly is cridly.

Many surnames are altered by an added s. Young becomes Youngs, and the family is called the Youngses. So of the names Hill, Moore, and others. Edgar is made Egdar.

A certain one, a scattered one, a very nod one. One here and there, few and far between. "A nod one" seems to be an odd one. "Very nod" is a frequent phrase.

I'll 'low. I'll allow. Used as in England we say, "I dare say," or "I suppose."

To step aside. To die, depart from life here.

A jacket colder. A very intelligible reading of the thermometer. The climate of the lower end of Greenspond harbour was said to be "a jacket colder" than the upper end, being more exposed. It was common, also, to indicate the degree of a change in weather by this phrase.

Very pretty pastime. A noticeable phrase, on account of its frequently strange application. A man getting a Prayer Book from me to use in his house, in a place where no reader held service and the clergyman's visits were sadly infrequent, said he was very glad to get it, because "reading the Prayer Book was very pretty pastime on Sundays."

As the saying is. A phrase continually recurring in conversation, when no current saying is quoted or referred to [1].

All as one. All the same.

---

[1] I have noticed some very amusing instances of this unmeaning use of phrases, but they were not general, and therefore not to be cited as current. One man continually brought into the midst of any thing he related the words "for instance," without any possible application to what he said. In like manner another used the words "in the mean time." I was once attending an aged sick man in a part of my mission far from Greenspond. There was neither church nor school-house, and public worship could only be performed in any dwelling-house chosen for the purpose. This time it was to be in the sick man's room, he being able to bear it, and desirous of joining in it. When the little congregation was assembled, and I was ready to begin my duties, the oldest son of the sick man entered and greeted the company with "Well, neighbours, how are you all upon an average?" I managed to keep my gravity, and no one attempted to ascertain the required average.

With all the veins of my heart.   A profession
of cordial willingness.

Alsó.   A laconic mode of saying that the   *That's*
speaker's feeling or opinion is the same as
that just before expressed by another person.
Probably a low Americanism.

To-morrow or the next day.   Any time not far
distant[2].

The other day.   As the phrase last named is
used indefinitely, so on the other hand this
always signifies the day before yesterday.

How d'ye get along? how d'ye make it out?
how do times govern with you?   Common
forms of inquiring how you do.   These phrases
no doubt originated in the sympathy of poor
people with their brethren whom they knew
to be struggling with poverty.

How do times govern in St. John's?   This question, always asked of any man lately returned
from the capital, is answered by recounting
the prices which fish and oil realized, and
those at which food and clothing were got in
return.

---

[2] At my first entering my mission, I visited all the people
to become acquainted with them, and was much distressed
by being asked in every house whether I would not come
again to-morrow or the next day, by which I understood the
definite time expressed.

Nautical phrases are in general use. Gaining any advantage over a man is called "getting to windward of him;" to be in declining circumstances is to be "going to leeward;" prospering is "making headway;" getting any work or business into order for progress is "getting under way;" to live meanly and parsimoniously is to "go very near the wind."

I have heard but very few proverbs in use amongst the fishermen of Newfoundland. One which I think is very expressive and characteristic I have already cited[3]. It was generally spoken with sufficiently pertinent application. There was a proverb more often used than any other, of which I must either believe it spoilt by misquotation, or else confess myself too dull to perceive its force: "We must live in hopes, supposing we die in despair." We have in Newfoundland a saying equivalent to the English one, "He robs Peter to pay Paul," and the Scotch, "He rives (tears) the kirk to theik (thatch) the choir." It is, "He sits in one end of the tilt and burns the other." This could only originate with people accustomed to live in wooden houses, and admirably expresses to their apprehension the folly of shiftless expedients. I

[3] Page 26, note.

once saw the literal fulfilment of this proverb. A poor thriftless family, too lazy to work, actually, while living in the forest, burned parts of one end of their house to warm themselves sitting at the other. Dean Ramsay, in his interesting "Reminiscences of Scottish Life and Character," gives two interpretations of his countrymen's proverb, "Ruse (praise) the fair day at e'en." The Dean reads it, "Give thanks at evening for the mercies of the past day;" while a friend whom he cites applies it thus: "Do not praise the day (or the season) till you have seen it closed." This has reminded me of a saying repeated to me in Newfoundland, which may be equally approved with Dr. Ramsay's quotation as he gracefully interprets it, and is far superior to the latter application. It is, "Always praise the bridge that carries you safe over." The beautiful words of Mr. Keble seem to me at once to interpret this proverb by paraphrase, and to improve its spirit:

> "Ready to give thanks and live
> On the least that Heaven may give."

A fisherman noted for industry and fair success, speaking to me with regret about a friend's slovenliness and neglect in business, said of himself and his sons, "We only keep above water *by dint of stupidity and hard work*, and how can he expect to thrive?" The words in italics, though I have not heard them since or before, cling to my memory as expressing with the pithy curtness of a proverb the means of many a dull plodding man's success,—not ready wit, but a principle which effects wonders in spite of natural deficiency,—honest industry.

Another very thrifty fisherman used often to say in reproof of profitless talk which hindered work, " Words fill no bags."

These few proverbs, not, I believe, generally known, seem to me worth noting here for the reason urged by one who a few years since collected the proverbial sayings of his country [4]. "If they are not registered, it is possible that they might have died with the tongue from which you took them, and so have been lost for ever."

A good deal of ready wit and clever repartee is common. An amusing case of the biter bit occurs to me as an instance. It was more innocent of any ill-feeling than sharp retorts are generally. A merchant whom I knew, very fond of joke and banter, heard one of my people name his eldest son's age, upon which he re-

---

[4] "The Proverbial Philosophy of Scotland," by Mr. Stirling of Kier.

marked, "Is it possible he is no older? Why, he must have been a great rogue to be so grey-haired already." The old fisherman, with scarcely so much changed expression as an arch look, quietly replied, "Well, I can hardly think that, or you'd have been grey yourself long years ago."

Many an amusing anecdote might be told of dull apprehension, which is so like perverse misapprehension and clever evasion, that you cannot be sure of which kind it is. I was told of one of my predecessors in Greenspond, that in trying with much earnestness and labour to correct the sordid temper of an aged parishioner, he cited as an exemplar the conduct of the martyr Cranmer. "He might have saved his life, John, if he would. All he need do to save himself from the fire would have cost him nothing, but he would not do wrong for any gain. It was only to write his name on a piece of paper, and he would not." The old man, much interested, exclaimed, "Why, he must have been a proper fool!"

Alas, how often are our words spent to as little purpose! I was once labouring to impress upon a man the duty of the flock to maintain its church and minister, and his own duty in particular to contribute to my yearly collection of dues. He replied that the Society (for the Propagation of the Gospel in Foreign Parts) maintained me, and that if my salary were not sufficient, the Society was to blame for having reduced it. To exculpate the Society, I asserted the ability of the flock, and showed how much the Society had done in wholly maintaining the mission for so many years, and paying its several successive ministers in that time no less a sum than so much. I now forget the time and sum. My argument resulted only in the man's astonished exclamation, "My! there's a sight of money the parsons had." I had but confirmed him in the common and most unreasonable notion that the parson is a rich man.

My brother, who held the mission of King's Cove, took a young woman from my flock to be his servant. She was a fair specimen of her class; sufficiently ready and active at work, but very dull to apprehend any instruction in higher things, and very little desirous of learning. My brother took much pains to improve her, chiefly by reading to her and catechizing her before the evening prayers of his family. Her seeming incapacity or indifference, it was hard to say which, was very discouraging, till one evening she said, "If you please, sir, there's one thing you read at prayers that I want to ask about." Delighted

at the dawn of intelligence, my brother inquired
her difficulty, but was soon disappointed in
learning that her curiosity sought no more than
an explanation of the "droll saying" in one of
the Psalms, "there is *little Benjamin*."

My own hopes have sometimes been excited
by a request for information, usually prefaced
with many apologies for making it: "I hope it's
no harm what I'm going to ask, sir, but I said
I'd ask you. Excuse my boldness." Then came
some question about a passage of Scripture. Too
commonly it proved to be only an idle inquisi-
tiveness upon some point which could have no
bearing upon their own faith and practice. I
have been taken aside from a journey, and de-
tained in a house by the way, solely to satisfy an
inquiry as to who were those sons of God that
allied themselves with the daughters of men.
One day, while on a journey in my last mission,
I saw a woman sitting outside her house, looking
very thoughtful over a book which I had lately
given her. I stayed to talk with her, and she
told me that she was in perplexity about the
subject on which she was reading. "I know it's
very stupid of me, sir; but I'm thinking and
stud'ing, and I can't make it out. And I've
asked Aunt Rachel too, and she's a very knowledgeable woman, but she can't resolve me."

The difficulty was first that she could not discover who was the mother of the Blessed Virgin. When I had helped her out of this trouble, she told me next that she could not find out to what tribe and family the Virgin belonged. I said, "The tribe of Judah, and the house of David." "Yes, sir, I know it's said she was of the house and lashens⁵ of David, but what I can't find out is which of Judah's sons she came of." It was now time to point out to her the unprofitableness of such inquiries, and direct her to more useful thoughts, which ended our conversation.

The class of "knowledgeable persons" to which Aunt Rachel belonged is a numerous and troublesome one. She, poor woman, was one of the least offensive. I dare say there is one or more of such persons in every flock. Not one of the many little communities in my mission was free from them; and too often they are the "dead flies (which) cause the ointment of the apothecary to stink." Their intention is not always mischievous, but their action is invariably such. Generally they are persons who can read a little, and perhaps also write, and are largely possessed with self-conceit. With little sense of

⁵ Lineage.

modesty and meekness they proclaim on every
side their superior knowledge and perception,
and are too often valued at their own estimation
by their more humble-minded neighbours.   Such
persons make it their especial province to interpret Scripture; and if their view differ from
an exposition given by their clergyman, this difference does but show their skill and capacity to
teach.   A person of this character once boasted
to me of an opportunity he had lately taken to
show himself vastly better informed than a neighbour whom I fear he despised.   He had convinced
his ill-taught friend ·that there was in the Bible
such a name for a boy as Brazilian.   I did not
gratify the man by declaring that I knew no
such name, but satisfied myself that he had mis-
read the name Barzillai.

The practice of choosing unusual names for
children from Holy Scripture, or from other
books, is well known amongst the poor every
where.   My people in Newfoundland were much
given to it, and often my utmost power of conjecture or invention was tried to find and give
the proper names to infants at their baptism.
The word spoken by the sponsors was often un-
like any known name, and when with difficulty
I discovered what it was intended for, it sometimes proved· so objectionable as to oblige me

to require a substitute. I was asked to name
one child Lo Ruhamah[6], and its mother was
much displeased that I disliked her choice. In
her family there had been both this name and
Lo Ammi. Jerusha, Abi, Keren-Happuch, and
other equally unusual names from Scripture were
often given. The names of evil characters were
as much in request as those of holy persons, and
it may be supposed the parents could not appreciate the feeling which objected to them. The
choice made from other sources was sometimes
more puzzling. Idgnīa was the name appointed
by one man to be given to his child. The
mother rightly hesitated to reject his choice
in his absence, so I taxed my memory to find
the name intended, and after much conjecture
adopted Eugenia. For another child I changed
Hemmony to Hermione. Pertilda was a mispronunciation of Matilda, and Familia of Pamela.
Diana, a very frequent choice, I rejected as
heathen, and substituted Dinah. A woman
whom I knew as Bertha was married years before as Bathsheba, while the register of her
baptism gave the name Beersheba. Once when
entering a baptism, the babe's mother gave her

---

[6] Hosea i. 6. Marginal interpretation, "not having ob-
tained mercy."

own name for entry as Blizer. Much puzzled
I asked her to spell it. " Well, sir," she replied,
"it's strange that you don't know it. Why
that's not all my name. I'm Anna Bliza."
This gave me a clue, and I entered her name
Annabella Eliza. The process of contraction
had been first, Bell Liza, and then Bliza. One
woman asked me to name her child Eeplet, and
I discovered the intention to be Hypolite. The
choice was her husband's, and he was a French-
man.

Once I found a child bearing the hateful
name of Cain. The poor child's story is painfully interesting. Born of evil parents, its
father disowned, and its mother abandoned it.
The father's sister took in the outcast and
adopted it, and after some time asked me to
baptize it. Upon putting the usual question
whether the child were already baptized, I discovered first by the hesitation of the sponsors
that something was wrong, and then by their
plain confession that its grandmother had baptized it, and in fancied appropriateness to its
outcast condition named it Cain. But the foster-
mother begged that I would neither regard that
baptism nor retain the odious name, for the
grandmother had acted in an outburst of ill-
temper, and the profanity of her act was so

E

gross that the young woman would fain regard it as null. I did as she desired, using the hypothetical form of baptism, and giving the child a name which was free from objection.

Irregular baptism ministered by all sorts of persons, though rarely by women, is very generally practised amongst the poor people in remote places, which seldom receive a clergyman's visit and ministrations. The children so baptized are always brought to the missionary when next he comes amongst them, and almost invariably the parents ask him to baptize them. I have, however, found a very few parents who felt satisfied with the baptism already received, and desired only the reception of the children into the Church.

At services held in dwelling-houses, where no church or school is in being, strange interruptions often arise, not only from the necessary presence of the younger members of the family, and the continuance during the service of some culinary processes, but also from the fact of the poor people's being unaccustomed to religious assembling, and not being under the peculiar solemn feeling which the very appearance of a sacred building serves to excite and foster. Immediately before beginning a service I have been disturbed by a woman near me, who intended no offensive familiarity, lifting my surplice to examine it, and remarking aloud upon it. My predecessor was once interrupted, in the midst of his sermon I believe, by the mistress of the house exclaiming to her grandchildren, "Lotte, hook out the lamp'. Jack, drive out the dog."

A poor man in my mission, whilst once reading the Church prayers, and a sermon for a little congregation where no reader was appointed, was similarly annoyed by an old woman in the chimney corner calling to some young ones, "My gracious, girls, I've forgot the loaf. Julia, go out to the next house and hang on the bakepot."

' i. e. trim the wick.

CHAPTER IV.

THE MISSIONARY AND HIS FLOCK.

THE Clergyman's rebuke of an erring parishioner is more often cleverly evaded than rudely or angrily rejected. One is often sent away sad and discomfited by the too ready and matter-of-course sort of assent given to all you say, your words seeming not to touch the sinner with any real feeling. They are not lost, assuredly; but oh, shall they reclaim the soul you love? However, the first case I now relate was not one of intentional repulse. A poor, very untaught young woman had been guilty of an offence for which it was needful that I should rebuke her. Long time passed before I got opportunity to do so, and she lived among persons who would, I feared, only lead her to think lightly of her fault. At last I did speak to her, and she met my rebuke in a manner which was at once touching from its artless simplicity, and such as to disarm me;

dropping a short curtsey, she said, "Yes, sir, bad thing I was to do it, sir, wasn't I?"

There was a man in my flock, whose general conduct was unsatisfactory and often needing rebuke, and who, though most respectful in manner, seemed in no way corrected by any admonition. I was one day standing by him at his work and speaking upon some common subject, when one of his customary oaths escaped him. Instantly he forestalled the expected rebuke by shaking his head remorsefully, and striking it a revengeful thump with his fist ; at the same time interspersing his discourse to me with words of self-reproach, "Bad man, Bill (thump)! What did you say that bad word for (thump)? Bad man!"

The free intercourse and intimacy which must be between the missionary and his people, when he has to spend days and nights as a guest in their houses, often place him in very strange positions, and bring out some amusing traits of character[1]. In the house of a family which

[1] Much tact is certainly required to sustain the missionary's proper character, but I can testify to the readiness of the flock, almost one and all, to recognize that character and respect it. They do so, certainly, not the less for the clergyman's accommodating himself, as far as is proper and possible, to their mode of life, and making himself familiar

always received and lodged me in my journeys to one extremity of my mission, was a very aged woman, the great-grandmother of the children there. She was a strangely taciturn person, and for a very long time I found no way to draw her into conversation. Occupied only in nursing a baby, and uttering almost continually a droning sound to lull her noisy charge to sleep or quietness, she seemed insensible to all that passed, hardly conscious of my presence, and, as far as I could judge, totally indifferent to the services which at each visit I held in the house. At length she proved that she had not been so altogether unobservant and regardless.

During one of my visits, being left alone with me, she broke silence, and here is our conversation, from which there sprang a gratifying, and,

with their cares and occupations. Some marked difference must all the while be rigidly preserved in his habits, from those of his entertainers; and this, so far from being offensive to them, is expected of him. As an instance, I may say that he should carefully avoid joining with his people in the use of spirits and tobacco. To readers in England I know this caution will seem a strange one, and unnecessary to be addressed to any one who is to be called to the ministry. Let them pardon me for saying, that without experience of the life I am depicting, they cannot appreciate the danger to a man so secluded from all refined associations, of sinking into a low deportment and degrading habits.

I trust, profitable intimacy. "I say, father, how old are you?" "I am twenty-nine." (She was a centenarian.) "Father, have you got any friends?" "Yes, I've a brother, the missionary at King's Cove." "Yes, yes, but haven't you got any friends in England?" "Yes, I have many kind friends in England." "But do they ever send you any thing?" "O yes, they write letters to me." "Ah, but don't they never send you nothing?" Her daughter and granddaughter had now come in, and were standing astounded at the poor old woman's loquacity, and shocked at the character of her questions. They tried to silence her, but she protested, "Now it's no harm what I'm saying, is it, father?" "No, indeed, it's not." I begged them not to interrupt her, and she resumed, "Well, now, people's friends does send 'em things sometimes, don't 'em?" Thus the dialogue proceeded for a little time, greatly amusing me. But more than that, it was the beginning of a free intercourse which enabled me to discover the poor woman's growing religious feeling and capacity for instruction. At a visit some time after I felt able with much thankfulness to receive her to the Holy Communion.

Very commonly two or three generations of a fisherman's family are dwelling under one roof.

In summer time, during the fishing season, servant men and women, and sharemen are there also. There were some houses in my mission in which two or three and thirty individuals thus lived together. One fisherman's house which I often visited, and in which I usually lodged for a night and day or longer, had, among its numerous inmates, five young married women and their children, and I think it was nothing unusual in that house for four cradles to be in requisition at the same time. The oldest inmate was a great-great-grandmother; four generations of her descendants being in the house with her, and her granddaughter's grandchildren in another house close by[2]. As all the women and grown children in a fisherman's household must be almost continually out of doors curing fish in the season, the care of the infants devolves greatly upon the aged people who are past labour. It is a hard, not to say cruel tax upon their failing energies, and they have sometimes complained to

[2] Families thus crowded together are not so living to save rent and taxes as in England, for in Newfoundland every man's house and land is his own freehold. It is to save labour and expense in building houses, for the economy of keeping but one fire and one table, and chiefly for the convenience of having all hands ready on the spot at all times for work.

me very movingly of the worry and distress it caused them. It is sad, indeed, to see the evening of life thus disturbed. This was the case both of the aged woman I have just now mentioned, and of her whose conversation I have related above. I was once both pained, and yet at the same time provoked to laugh at the efforts I saw this person making to quiet a baby who was squalling vigorously. The poor old nurse sat alone in the sun, rocking her chair vehemently, or in Newfoundland parlance, "venomously," and with ludicrously brief alternations, was coaxing the squaller, and denuding and flogging it.

Much unaffected simplicity of manner and childlike teachableness marked the character of some of the best among my people. A very fine old man, from Christchurch in Hampshire, who always seemed to rejoice in an hour's talk with his minister, one day rose from his seat in the schoolroom of the place in which he lived,—that room was both the church and school there,— and coming to the desk where I was preparing to read the prayers, began to talk of his knowledge of the New Version of the Psalms. Seeming quite unconscious or heedless of the presence of the assembling congregation, he placed his hands behind him like a boy in class, and repeated to me the whole of the Ninetieth Psalm

in verse. In the tenth stanza the sense is in-
complete without the following one. The old
man, however, made the usual cadence at the
words " to eighty we arrive," without suspicion of
the incompleteness.

I have spoken of the love of money as an evil
too generally prevalent in my flock at Greenspond; but I ever felt in dealing with this evil
that they had more sore temptation to it than
most men in England experience. Persons of
this class at home, and like them little raised
by education, are not used to the possession of
any store. Most men of wealth in England in-
herited much, and the increase of their possessions
is almost a natural process; parsimony is therefore in them an error, very different in degree
from the closeness and hoarding of my fishermen,
whose little hoard is the fruit of their own hard
labour and scant living. The converse holds
equally true. The liberality of most monied
men at home is ·a far easier virtue than that of
these poor Newfoundlandmen, and may be in
some cases only an exemplification of the proverb
that "what easily comes easily goes." With
this consideration in mind I greatly value any
evidence which can be produced of cheerful
giving to good uses on the part of my late flock,
and I would beg my readers to take into account

the faults of habit and education which must in their case have been overcome, while I relate to them some of the efforts which have been made by the flock at Greenspond.

The mission owes its establishment, and its maintenance since the appointment of its first clergyman in 1830, to the bounty of the venerable Society for the Propagation of the Gospel [3]. But twenty years before this there was a strong effort and a large outlay of money on the part of the then small population to obtain and secure to themselves and their children those religious privileges which had been lost to them by their emigration from England to this desolate country. It. is now about fifty years since the people of Greenspond Island agreed together to build a church there, and many of their brethren on the neighbouring small islands helped them [4]. They

[3] Even before 1830 I believe the Society employed and paid schoolmasters and readers in two or three places of the mission.

[4] I believe these poor people had no other encouragement to this work than a vague trust that if they built a house for prayer and preaching, a teacher would somehow be found or sent for them. This seems to be evidenced by the fact, told me by one of the original contributors, that when the church was built a meeting of the people consulted whether they should try to get a Methodist Teacher or a Clergyman of the Church. A large majority declared their firm adherence to the Church of their fathers in England.

very soon erected a church, a not very suitable
building certainly, but very creditable to the religious feeling of those who were thus seeking
again the God of their fathers. I say *seeking
Him again*, for by their own statement it is
sadly evident that the whole people were fear-
fully immoral, and it might be said of them very
generally that God was not in all their thoughts.
Sunday was observed only as the day for putting
in order all the fishing gear used in the previous
week or required for the week ensuing. The
merchants' stores were open till mid-day, and
the fishermen then took their salt and made
other purchases. The clergyman who first had
charge of this mission, the Rev. N. A. Coster,
had to entreat the master-fishermen to allow
their servants time to attend the church; and as
a proof of how little the honour due to God in
His house was felt, I may mention that the rum-
bottle was passed from hand to hand in the
upper gallery of the church during the time of·
Divine Service.

At various times since this first willing offering, the people of Greenspond have had occasion
to spend money for religious uses in large proportion to their means. That first church was
twice or three times altered and enlarged, and a
rearrangement and improvement of the interior,
which was effected by the zeal of the first mis-

ST. STEPHEN'S CHURCH AND PARSONAGE, GREENSPOND.

sionary, was very expensive to the people. Lastly, in the time of my holding of the mission, that church was demolished, and a large and handsome one built at a cost of several hundred pounds, contributed chiefly by the fishermen of the place [5]. -

But these were, it may be said, only spasmodic efforts, the temporary result of excitement. It is more important to show the existence of a regular systematic self-taxation by the people for their Church's. support. This, I am happy to say, I can do. The clergymen who were my predecessors received a full and sufficient maintenance from the Society for the Propagation of the Gospel, and therefore had not occasion to demand such large general contributions from their flock as became necessary when on my appointment I received only half the stipend which had been previously provided from the Society [6]. Still, from the first, a yearly collection was made by those clergymen, in addition to payments made to the churchwardens for the expenses of the public services in church. As nearly as I could ascertain, the people's usual

[5] See Appendix A.
[6] This reduction was made by a rule applying to all the missionaries of the Society in Newfoundland who should be appointed in and after the year 1849.

and regular contributions were about 45*l.* yearly. In my own time their payments gradually became larger and more general, and the recognition of the duty of the flock to maintain its pastor, slowly and with difficulty, but progressively, gained a hold upon the people's mind and will. Owing to the heavy expense incurred by them in building their new church, and by reason of a large part of my collection being appropriated by the Diocesan Church Society to the annual payment of readers in my mission, the average of my own receipts in augmentation of my stipend during ten years was but 20*l.* per annum. Upon the completion of the church, however, an immediate effort was made by the flock to correct this deficiency of my stipend, and an additional quarterly collection for charitable uses was willingly undertaken [7]. At length, upon the appointment of my successor in the mission in June 1860, the people voluntarily accepted the entire burden of their clergyman's maintenance, and released the venerable Society from any longer continuance of its bounty to them [8].

[7] This quarterly collection was for, 1. The Society for the Propagation of the Gospel's Missions to the Heathen; 2. The Society for Promoting Christian Knowledge; 3. Clergy's Widows and Orphans' Fund; 4. General Orphan Asylum of the Church of England in St. John's, Newfoundland.

[8] See Appendix B.

The history of the several small churches built
in other stations of the mission is in many particulars similar to what I have related of that
on Greenspond Island. They were the smaller
offerings to God's glory of smaller flocks; but I
doubt not they were as large in proportion to
the means of the builders, and were the fruits
and evidence of a like spirit.

On Pinchard's Island the first church was a
store, purchased and dedicated by the people to
its sacred use. It was consecrated, I believe, by
the late Bishop Inglis of Nova Scotia. Old and
unsuitable from the first period of its adaptation,
it had become, when I saw it, almost a ruin.
The building of a handsome and substantial new
church for this flock was the first work of the kind
committed to me. One fishing crew gave more
than 70l. towards it; another nearly 50l., and the
rest in like proportion to their means. Among
the contributors was one man, now no more on
earth, whom I have reason especially to remember as a bright example of faith and good deeds.
He, with his sons, purchased a large vessel for
the sealing voyage and the Labrador fishery, and
this for some time afterwards obliged him to
practise very careful economy. He had already
given money freely to assist the building. Upon
my first seeing him after his purchase he pro-

mised to give 10*l.* more, if the vessel were successful on her first voyage. Meeting me again a few days after, he referred to his recent promise, and retracted the terms; "For," said he, "I have the 10*l.* now by me, and if I keep it, and our vessel does badly, I shall certainly be tempted to spend it, and let the church go short. You shall therefore have it now at once."

The story of the origin of the church at Swaine's Island, is to me the most interesting of all.

The original settlers on this very small place were two Englishmen, in great poverty, and with large families to maintain. Each kept a fishing-boat, manned by hired servants or sharemen, their own sons being too young for work [9]. For a long time their struggle for life was a hard one, and their success was not at the first equal. The man whose crew first began to prosper was from Ringwood in Hampshire. He left home young without knowledge of writing or reading. But despite his ignorance and long separation from good associations his heart yearned for the church-going habits of his childhood, and

---

[9] Both these families have thriven, and are now numbered among the most substantial planters in Newfoundland.

his were not idle yearnings[1]. One of his fishing crew was an Englishman already advanced in years, who could read fairly. My friend—for in his old age I knew him, and as a friend I love to remember him—my friend said to this servant man, "John, thee canst read. It seems a sad unchristian way for my boys to grow up without learning. Do thee stop ashore and teach the children, and I'll pay thee thy wages as thof[2] thee went in the boat." John agreed, and undertook also at his master's desire to read the Church's prayers in his house every Sunday. The benefit of this teaching and reading was cheerfully extended to the neighbour's family. When this had been some time continued, the author of the arrangement became discontented, and consulted for an improvement with John and his neighbour, who was now to be a partner with him in the good work.

The frequent disturbance of the Sunday ser-

---

[1] It is pleasant to trace all the beneficent fruits of this good man's religious acts back to their origin in the holy influence of a pious mother's early teaching. After he had passed threescore and ten years his mother was yet living in Hampshire, and received a yearly gift of money remitted to her by him. At ninety years of age she still continued her accustomed walk of four miles' distance to the church, and the same distance returning.

[2] The common pronunciation of "though."

F

vices in the house, caused by domestic matters, and the presence of fretful infants, determined them to get timber from the forests and build a small church. This was effected, and the building was a few years afterwards visited and consecrated by the Bishop of Nova Scotia, and the Reader was by him duly licensed. Before I left Greenspond this church, grown old and decayed, was taken down, and a new one far larger and better was being erected by the flock, and I believe it is now completed and consecrated.

The person whose endeavours for God's service and his brethren's good I have been dwelling upon, is not unjustly reputed a keen and careful dealer, of perhaps too saving habits. Being such, his acts of devotion to God and liberality to man must have cost him the greater effort, and prove the nobler victory over self. I have been privy to many unostentatious acts of charity, which were probably unknown to those who noted and condemned his parsimony. Let me be excused for digressing now and again from this narrative of the history of the Churches, while I adduce one or two instances of his and other such poor men's benevolence.

An Italian man once visited my mission, seeking help under very distressing circumstances. Some persons gave him a rude rebuff, which he may perhaps have deserved, but which they were not justified in offering. My own impression, after careful consideration, was that his tale was true, and he deserving. Be this as it may, the conduct of my aged friend at Swaine's Island claims admiration. The stranger came to him and offered credentials for examination. The old man could not read them. No person was near with whom he could consult. He reasoned, therefore, with himself thus: "If I give to this man I may help an impostor. My money was earned by hard work, and he may be a worthless vagabond. But again, I have no way to prove his tale false, and know nothing against him but my own suspicion. If I give to him and he is false, I do it innocently, and the sin is wholly his. If I send him empty away, I may grieve at the great day for not feeding the hungry nor caring for the stranger. Yet if I give to him, and my neighbours discover it, some will not fail to laugh and say that fools and their money are easily parted. Shall I regard God or man? He is my Judge, and my reward is sure." This is, as nearly as I can give it, the old man's own account to me of his reasoning on the case. He was about to give four dollars (20s.) to the stranger, but considering that the money was for use of a traveller, he substituted

a sovereign (24s.) " because English gold would
pass any where."

A more affecting instance of the same virtue
was shown by a poorer and a less instructed
man, in a very trying situation. He lived in
Cat Harbour, a place which was visited by me
and my predecessors seldom oftener than twice a
year. Between those visits no man read any
prayers, or attempted any public religious obser-
vance of the Lord's day. In truth, no one there
could read sufficiently well to do so. The man
whose conduct I am to relate, had gone through
a peculiarly hard struggle for life. His family
had been a very large one, of which only two
children were sons, and able when they grew up
to help him. Many a tale of want and labour
cheerfully endured has he told me with no word
of repining. In his old age he had attained to
comfort and independence, but possessed no store
laid by, or as he would express it, he was nothing
beforehand. His house lay in the path of all
travellers on the shore to and from the northward of my mission, and as it was the chief one
there, and he was well known as the patriarch
of the place, his visitors were many and his
hospitality was unfailing. In 1852 his charity
was severely tested. About sixty vessels on
the sealing voyage, carrying crews averaging

about forty men in each vessel, were wrecked or abandoned on the coast of my mission. Many of these crews came ashore to the northward of his dwelling, and making their way overland towards Greenspond, stayed by the way at any house which would receive them and afford refreshment. Several troops of men were entertained at the old man's house. Still they came, and his wife feared with reason that her household would soon be sorely straitened by providing food for so many strangers. One crew more came in, and she looked despairingly at her husband. The wrecked party assured her they were the last company coming up the shore: but so others also had spoken, and now she doubted them. She appealed to the old man: "Matthew, what *be* we to do?" His reply was, "Hang on the kettle, and get the men some bread." The poor old woman went to their little stock, and returned with five pounds' weight of bread in her apron—just half of all that remained to her house—and gave it to the strangers, little knowing when her family could get a fresh supply. The Arctic drift-ice was on the coast, close set in by the east wind; it had been so for weeks past, and might remain for any length of time to come, forbidding all

communication with other places. Greenspond
and the other settlements near were all equally
distressed, having in them more than two thousand
strangers, to be supported out of the small store
provided for our own population only.   Happily
the good old man and his family were not suffered to want; relief was sent in time, and he
has since gone to his reward.

Before I left Greenspond mission, a very good
school-house was built in Cat Harbour, at the
joint expense of the people and the Government
Board of Education.   The school was in opera-
tion and well attended, and the master read
divine service publicly in the school-room every
Sunday.   A happy change this in the circumstances of the place, and in this, I think, no one
felt more real and deep satisfaction than the
worthy old man I have named.   It had been for
long years the desire of his heart to see this
work carried out, and his pleasure at its completion was something beautiful to observe, though
he was now so crippled by hard labour, and
enfeebled by age, that he could not even once
attend the service.   The part performed by the
people of Cat Harbour in getting their school-
house built, may serve well to show their for-
wardness to do according to their power for their

souls' good, and to illustrate some of the difficulties which impede missionary work as well as
all other labour upon a coast like this.

In October 1855, sixteen men, being one person from every household in Cat Harbour, took
the two largest boats in the place for a voyage of
more than sixty miles to get timber for their
proposed school-house. Within a week they cut
and conveyed on board the boats more than 180
timbers. Then came bad weather, with strong
wind against them on their homeward course,
and a very heavy sea off Cape Freels, which they
must pass. Three times they attempted to get
home, and as often had to bear up and wait.
At length, after more than three weeks' delay,
they had to discharge their cargo of timber and
lay up their boats in Greenspond for the winter,
thus submitting to twelve months' postponement
of the building. The disappointment and difficulty did not spoil their temper, or cool their
zeal. At the same time the next year, which
was their first season of leisure, they again went
after the timber, and on this occasion they succeeded in conveying it to its destination.

In that same season of disasters when the
strangers in distress were so charitably entertained out of the scanty store of that good man

at Cat Harbour[3], a person at Fair Island as aged as he, but less infirm, performed a labour of brotherly kindness for the relief of two perishing men which deserves to be recorded. The drift-ice, then close set in upon the shore by the continual east wind, had upon it great numbers of seals, and men, women, and boys from all the settlements upon the shore went out to take them. One day, when very many people from Greenspond were at this work, the wind veered off the shore, and driving away the ice, made it hardly possible for them to return to land. Several persons remained for great part of the night following upon some rocks in much distress, till some men put off in punts from the shore, and with great difficulty reached them and brought them home. Two men who had been out since five o'clock the morning previous, altogether failed of getting to any land, and to ward off that fatal lethargy which overtakes per-

---

[3] His act of charity is not adduced as a solitary instance of this virtue among the flock. Far otherwise is the truth, and the troubles of that "spring of the wrecks," as the time is always named, called forth many a bright example of that consideration for the poor and needy, which shall be remembered, I trust, for the deliverance of my people in their own hour of trial.

sons exposed to extreme cold, they were obliged
to continue walking upon the ice throughout the
night. They had taken with them in the morning only a little biscuit [4], which was eaten early
in the day. In the night they strove to stay
their craving stomachs by gnawing ice. For
thirty-one hours these two men were upon the
ice before their deliverer found them. In the day
they had been labouring to get seals, in the
night they were enduring the terrors of immi-
ment death. At the end of this time the old
man of whose kindness I am to speak came upon
them lying exhausted upon the ice. They were
nearer to Fair Island than to Greenspond, so he
determined to get them to his own home.
Taking one man upon his back, he carried him
a short distance, and setting him down, returned
for the other. In this way he continued to carry
them for four hours, till finding his strength as
well as the daylight failing, he sent home a little
boy who was with him to get help. Happily,
some young men had at that time returned to
Fair Island from their day's work, and they at
once launched a punt into a lake of water formed
by the separation of the ice from part of the
shore, which reached nearly to the place where

[4] Sailor's bread.

the poor men were now lying. They came and carried one of the sufferers on board their punt and then returned for the other, but just as they came to him his life departed. Fearing to get themselves into danger by longer delay, the young men left his corpse upon the ice. The aged man who had so laboured to save two fellow-men from perishing, seemed afterwards quite unconscious of having done any thing worthy of notice. Doubtless his deed is therefore more precious in the sight of his Father which seeth in secret [5].

[5] See Appendix C.

CHAPTER V.

THERE were a few families in my mission whose position claims peculiar sympathy. They were salmon-fishers, living, by necessity of their occu- ·pation, each family apart from all neighbours, and secluded more than all others from the Church's ministrations of grace. A salmon-catcher hires or purchases the exclusive right of fishing, at some brook far up the country, from the merchant who first took possession of it. And there he lives alone, in summer catching and pickling salmon, in winter setting and tend-ing traps for foxes, martens, otters, bears, and other animals whose fur is valuable. If he can, he may, and probably does read the Church's prayers with his family on Sunday; but so un-wearied and dull is life in such isolation, that one of these men who did so observe his religious duties told me he once lost count of the days, and was for a long time in uncertainty whether

he were observing Sunday or another day.   One
family in which no one was able to read kept
the weekly day of rest with pious exactness, but
they lamented to me very movingly the weari-
someness of a day in which they would fain be
religiously occupied, but could only eat, drink,
and sleep, and wish it past.   I visited these
families as often as I could, but, alas, far too
seldom for their need: in some summers once,
not at all in others, and only on two occasions
in winter.   No where was my visit more highly
valued, and perhaps no where was there more
manifest improvement made by the little opportunity afforded.   Truly

" Scantness is aye Heaven's might."

One of these families consisted only of a man
and his wife, both getting aged, and a young
man, the woman's son by a former marriage.
This couple had married late in life, and had
one only child, a daughter: how dear to them in
the wilderness, the parents of an only child in
an ordinary station of life cannot judge!   They
could not read, but she was more to them than
learning, more than all other society could be.
At eight years old she fell sick and died, I believe without the presence of a doctor, and no
minister was there to pray with her and console

the bereaved parents. This was some years before my first visit to them, but that sore grief was yet very fresh in their hearts, and it was my office to console and instruct them. The affliction was fruitful of good. The father became after a few visits from me a Communicant, and to the last of my acquaintance with him his behaviour seemed to be that of a consistent and earnest Christian.

At my first visit to the house of another salmon-fisher, I formed acquaintance with a venerable man whom I shall ever love to remember. He was an Englishman, father of the fisherman, and was nearly eighty years old, but still very active. His wife, though several years younger, was much more feeble. When I knew them well, the mutual affection of the aged couple, and the reverence and love which the whole family showed towards them, was something beautiful to see. After a respectful greeting at my entrance on this first visit, the old man quietly regarded me awhile, and then exclaimed, "Thank God, I see a Minister in my house once more. It is twelve years since I saw one here." We talked together, and he soon asked me whether I was in Priests' Orders, and could give him the Lord's Supper. I replied in the affirmative to both questions, and again he thanked

God. "For," said he, "twelve years ago Parson
—— was here, and I wished then to receive it,
but he was a deacon and could not give it.
Twelve years I've waited, sir. But I shall receive it now." I inquired, with surprise, how
he with no instructor had learnt to desire it;
and he replied, "I've a good instructor here,
sir," showing me a large Common Prayer Book
published by the Society for Promoting Christian
Knowledge. I found that it was his habit every
day to retire for an hour or longer to his bed-
room with his Bible and Prayer Book, and not
merely to read but to really study them. And
the Church's exhortations in the Communion
Office had been, under God's direction, a sufficient guide to the desire and the preparation for
the Lord's table[1]. He seemed to regard the
Sacrament truly as a help and means to holy
living; not as a mere figurative representation,
nor yet a cloak for unrepented sin. He had, as
might be expected, taken care to instruct his
wife, and she too was prepared to receive her
first Communion, and did so with him the next

[1] This struck me as a practical enforcement of Bishop
Wilson's admonition to the careful and distinct reading
of these exhortations by the clergy ministering in Church.
See his "Short and Plain Introduction to the Lord's Supper." Note in loc.

day. I visited these people many times afterwards, and usually found the old man prepared
with some questions upon the chapters he had
recently read in his Bible. They were ever
profitable questions, affecting faith and duty. I
had not to complain of him as of some, that he
was curious about things of no importance to
his eternal good.

A short account of a summer passage to these
two last-named stations made in a boat in 1854,
will afford a very fair notion of the difficulties
which commonly attend the clergyman's work.
I had gone to the home of the former family
with the intention of returning thence to
Greenspond, but some business brought the
salmon-fisher of the latter station to the same
place, and I was very glad to go with him to
his home, upon his promising to carry me to
Greenspond afterwards. These two stations
were far separate, but I hoped to go from one
to the other in a day. There was, however, a
fresh and increasing breeze nearly ahead, and
after a day's beating against it we were yet
far from our destination. Fearing more wind,
and not liking to overstrain the boat, which
was very old and leaky, the fisherman proposed to me to run into a small bay near us,
and come to anchor for the night. We did so,

and as we were lowering sail heard a gun, and looking about saw a punt with two persons rowing away from us round a point of land. It was a pleasing surprise to find some one near us where we knew of no neighbour, and we at once determined to seek out these people on the shore, and get better quarters for the night than our boat afforded. With a little trouble we found the party, consisting of a man and his wife and little boy from Fair Islands, who had come up the bay looking for birds, seals, or any thing else that could be shot, fish being then scarce on the outside. Their only shelter for night was a shed, such as is called a back-tilt, made of a punt's sail strained along the ground on one side, and supported at an angle of about forty-five degrees from the ground by stakes. The ends are walled in with boughs, and the whole front is open; whence its name, being a back shelter only. In front of the tilt there was a fire burning, with a kettle hung over it to boil. We were kindly and gladly welcomed, and I was not sorry to see the boiling kettle and preparations for a meal. The gun we had heard was fired at a seal, which our host got by walking up to his armpits into the water. The inner parts of the seal were cooked for supper, and I was very thankful for a share. I had at that time

tasted no unsalted meat for about two months.
After supper and a brief evening service we
made preparations for rest. The man and his
two sons who were my own party had to dispose
themselves on the earth outside the tilt, and lie
subject to be attacked by nippers, musquitos,
and other vermin during the night, and to a
frost in the morning. Room was cheerfully
spared for me inside the little tent, which afforded only just sufficient space for my entertainers and myself to lie down. The bed was of
boughs, and my pillow was a sealskin filled with
biscuit, commonly and rightly named hard bread.
I left these kind people, without arousing them,
at daybreak, and easily finished the passage to
the salmon-brook that day. On the return
voyage to Greenspond in the same boat, we were
again kept out a night. This time it was for
lack of wind, and in a place where we could not
anchor. I turned in to lie down in the cuddy of
the boat, but the nippers and musquitos were so
busy at me that sleep was not possible, and I
soon turned out again, and took charge of the
helm for the remainder of the night to keep
myself from dropping to sleep in the damp night
air.

Many families leave their usual dwellings in
the fall of the year, and remove for the winter

into the woods far up the country, where they remain till nearly the end of May. Their purpose is to fell and square timber, saw board, cleave coopers' staves, make birch hoops for casks, or build boats. Their houses in the woods, named winter tilts, and required only to serve for one winter's use, are of very simple construction. A small space is cleared of all wood except two opposite trees, growing at such a distance apart as is a suitable length for the house. A longer [1] is extended from one to the other of these trees, and seized to them at the proper height for the roof ridge. The four walls are made of the trunks of trees set close together perpendicularly. Slender young trees are used for rafters, and these are covered with fir rinds to form a roof. The floor is made of longers, a flat rock forms the hearth, and the chimney is simply a space left uncovered in one end of the roof. No window is made or needed, the chimney admitting sufficient light. The chinks between the sticks of which the walls are made are caulked, or as these people say, chintzed, with moss. No labour is spent in dressing any timber in the tilt; even the rind is kept on; only the

---

[1] Such a stick as would be used for the horizontal rail of a fence.

A WINTER TILT.

longers of the floor are dubbed flat with an adze.
One end of the interior is partitioned off by a
punt's sails, or some other simple contrivance,
and serves the family for bed-chambers.

Commonly two or three families settle their
winter habitations near together for the sake of
society, but it is not suitable for many to be in
company, because each party of workmen needs
a large range of forest to get the timbers they
require. The winter settlements therefore are
small, numerous, and widely scattered. No roads
or paths connect them, but the traveller who
would visit them must make his way, sometimes
upon the ice by the shore, sometimes through
the wild unbroken forest, penetrable only in
winter, when musquitos are gone, when the
morass is frozen, and the scrubby undergrowth
in the woods is buried in deep snow.

A special equipment is necessary for such a
journey. Its chief particulars are strong coarse
cloth trousers and a reefer jacket, a fur cap with
laps to cover the ears, blanketing cuffs in lieu
of gloves for the hands, gaiters of the same
material, mocassins, which are a kind of leather
sock, in lieu of shoes, and Indian raquets or
snow shoes, which, by their covering a large surface as you tread, enable you to walk on soft
deep snow without sinking. Added to this dress

there should be a sealskin bag hung by slings
upon the shoulders, and containing a change of
clothing and some food—if the traveller be a
missionary, some books also and wine for the
Holy Communion[2];—a rug for lying upon at
night; a gun, with powder-flask and shot-belt,
for killing partridges, and sometimes other game;
a spiked stick to try the thickness and strength
of ice; and a hatchet slung to the waist to cut
wood for firing, if ever the traveller should be
obliged to bivouac in the forest for a night.

In such guise I twice made a tour of my people's
winter settlements, and it would be well if the
clergyman of such a mission could do this every
winter.   My own health so thoroughly broke
down that I could not continue the practice.
The journey, with only a day and night's tarry
at each station, occupied three weeks, and was
attended with great fatigue and hardship.   The
people in their winter quarters have much less
ability to lodge a guest than in their more con-
venient permanent dwellings; and that I might
not deprive women of their proper rest, I habi-
tually refused the bed they offered me, and lay
at night upon the longers by the fireside.

A narrative of one of these journeys may be

---

[2] Unless I were alone this bag was carried for me.

·interesting. - It will not be necessary to detail my proceedings at each place of my tarrying. Of course in each I read the services of the Church, and preached; always addressing these small congregations extempore; and if any communicants were present, I also celebrated the Lord's Supper.

My journey was begun from Greenspond on the 2nd of February, when the surface of the water for many miles off the coast was frozen, so that it was possible to walk from island to island, and thence in to the main shore, in almost any part of my mission. Beginning with visiting two or three of the most northern stations on the shore, I proceeded from thence across the country inside the coast, to the winter settlements westward, and thence returned down the shore to Greenspond. My first real difficulty was likely to be fatal to the lives of myself and two young men who were with me. They had kindly volunteered to accompany me from Pinchard's Island to Deadman's Bay and back again to their starting-place. In Seal Cove, below Cat Harbour, we all three together broke through some deceitful ice, and had some difficulty in getting out again. My companions were more thoroughly wet than I was. Our outside clothes froze stiff and hard upon us as soon as they were exposed to the wind, and my companions' boots had water in them. This misadventure did not deter us from proceeding to cross Deadman's Bay upon the ice, which was there firm and good. Half-way across the Bay the ice proved thinner, and still thinner, the further we went onwards. The young men thought the fatigue of returning more than we could bear in our half-frozen condition, and so nothing was before us but the dangerous attempt to reach the opposite land, over ice which proved weaker, and bent more alarmingly, under our feet at every step [4]. We walked apart to disperse our weight upon its surface. Soon it became too weak for walking, and we crept upon hands and knees, and to our horror we saw that between us and the shore was open water, with only here and there a loose piece of hard ice afloat in it. A breeze blowing towards us forbad all hope of our voices being heard ashore, and there was not even a dog about who might perhaps see us, and barking at us, give warning of our approach. One of my companions, now summoning courage for a bold venture, rose to his feet, and first bidding me expect his return with help, he bounded swiftly and lightly over

[4] Salt water ice is not brittle as that of fresh water. It yields very perceptibly to the pressure of any weight without breaking.

the little skim of ice till he could leap to one of
the floating pieces, and by thus jumping from
one of these to another, he gained the land.
From one of the houses he got two pieces of
board, and with them returned to fetch us.   One
board he laid upon the ice, and upon it he crept
along carrying the other.   Thus using the boards
by turns he reached us, and in the same mode
we got to land.   The people on shore did their
utmost to welcome and refresh us, but they were
in sad poverty, and had no change of clothes
to lend my young men, and no other food than
tea and molasses, and bread without butter.
We thawed and dried our clothes as we stood in
them.   The people told us that where we had
been walking was open water the day before.
After I had read the Evening Prayers, and
preached with the few neighbours who had assembled in the house, the poor man and his
wife who had received us insisted upon my ac-
cepting their own and only bed for the night.
Extreme cold, and the wretchedness of the bed
soon, however, obliged me to rise, and I spent the
night sitting with them by the fire.   When we
departed the next morning the ice was become
firm, and we travelled without difficulty.

It may be asked, why need a visit to this
place be made at such a season of difficulty and

danger?   The reason was that I could never but
once get a passage thither by water in the summer, and then I was obliged to spend a night by
the way in a boat at anchor off Cape Freels.
The boat was so small as to afford absolutely no
shelter, and I slept on the gang-boards[5], wrapt
up in the foresail.   My detention for the night
was caused by failure of the wind.   The journey
to Deadman's Bay on foot round the shore was
so toilsome, that with no better lodging and
refreshment than could be afforded there it was
scarcely to be thought of, especially by the missionary, who had afterwards many days of fatigue
and privation to pass before he could reach home
and rest.   One chief impediment to a journey by
land between Cape Freels and Deadman's Bay
was the several wide brooks that must be crossed.
These I usually waded. One of the largest of
these was in the way of my visits to Cat Harbour, and sometimes after travelling so far, I
have had to return with my purpose defeated,
and the poor people denied a visit which they
expected, and would have greatly valued.   I
remember being once sadly disappointed in this
way, and longing to let my poor flock know that
they were not uncared for, I took a card from my

---

[5] A partial deck covering the fish lockers.

pocket, and wrote upon it a brief notice of my defeated attempt. The card was fixed to the top of a stake by the brook side, and was soon afterwards observed by one of the people, as I hoped it might be. After the winter visit to Deadman's Bay related above, I was obliged to neglect that place, and did not go thither again for six years.. If a missionary resided nearer to them, say at Pinchard's Island, with only the northern part of the. present Greenspond Mission in his care, the journey or water passage to these places would be in his case a far less trying duty. My purpose now, however, is not to advocate the peculiar requirements of this mission, so much as to show what is the nature and difficulty of missionary work in such places generally.

To resume my narrative. Having returned as far as Pinchard's Island, where my companions were to leave me, I found two men about to travel to Indian Bay, and with them I took my journey up the country, and visited houses in Indian Bay, Trinity Bay, Locker's Bay, and six separate places in Freshwater Bay. In each place I found some man cheerfully willing to leave his work for a day or longer, and be my escort to the next settlement. There was much of interesting incident throughout the journey, but I fear to be too prolix in the relation.

At one house I found two families so poorly provided with food, that they could offer me only the coarsest quality of sailor's bread, and boiled tea with molasses. Of course I accepted it with the feeling and the expression of gratitude, knowing it to be the best and only food they had. On my return a few days later I called again to see these poor people, intending only to speak a few words of kindness, and at once pass on. They pressed me to take refreshment, and quickly spread their table with good bread and *butter*, tea and *sugar*. I accepted the kindness without remark upon the change, but wondered much how it had been managed. From some of their neighbours afterwards I learnt, that in expectation of my return the poor women had travelled several miles to another house to borrow or beg better food for me.

At a house in Freshwater Bay I found an aged man whom I had long been visiting in Greenspond, now become very weak and bedridden. As soon as he heard my voice in the house, he said to his wife, "Thank God, Mr. Moreton's come. I hope I shall die before he goes again." He was eager to see me, and I went to his bedside and prayed with him. I spoke of the Lord's Supper, of which we had often before conversed, and he expressed a desire

for it. "In the morning," said I, "you shall
receive it." I left him for the night to pray and
prepare himself, and at six o'clock the next
morning we found that he was gone where
Sacraments are not needed. I remained three
days at this house for the old man's burial.

From Freshwater Bay I started with a man
for my guide and companion to walk to Bloody
Bay. Travelling had now become very difficult
from an unusual cause. Many successive days
of mild, or, as it is expressively called, *soft* weather, had thawed away all the snow upon the
barrens and spare-grown woods, and small brooks
or rivulets were running in all directions. My
guide was a man soon cowed by difficulty, and
this day he was also unwell. We journeyed over
some thick-wooded mountain-ridges into a large
open country, over which we proceeded a few
miles till we came to a wide open brook. By
walking some distance along its bank we found
a large tree uprooted by wind, lying across and
bridging the brook. Upon this tree we crept
over. Some way further on a second brook gave
us trouble. The ice upon this was not wholly
gone, but was broken from its banks. We got
over this too with difficulty. A third brook
quite open was too much for my guide's almost
exhausted spirits. I desired him therefore to

turn back with me, that we might at least get to
the woods for shelter. We walked on our
return till the night was grown too dark for
seeing our way, and then we halted and set about
making the best quarters we could for a night's
rest. Our *back-tilt* was made with my bearskin
rug strained for its back and roof, and sides
were made as usual with boughs. Fronting the
open part we made a large fire, and under the
shelter we laid a bed of spruce twigs. Two partridges which I had shot in the day were cooked
for our supper, helped by a little rill of good water
which I found close by. Owing to the smallness
of its covering our tilt would only receive our
heads and shoulders, while our legs lay outside.
In that night the weather changed. First a
slight frost skimmed over the little brooks with
thin ice, and then a very heavy fall of snow
covered the ground to a depth of three feet in
the quiet woods, and eighteen inches in the open
places where the wind beat and hardened it.
The heat of our fire melted the snow as it fell in
our neighbourhood, and that which lay upon the
tilt leaking in through the boughed ends made
us thoroughly wet and uncomfortable. In the
morning we found that our halting-place was in
a spot which we knew to be about two miles
from some houses, but so difficult was the travel-

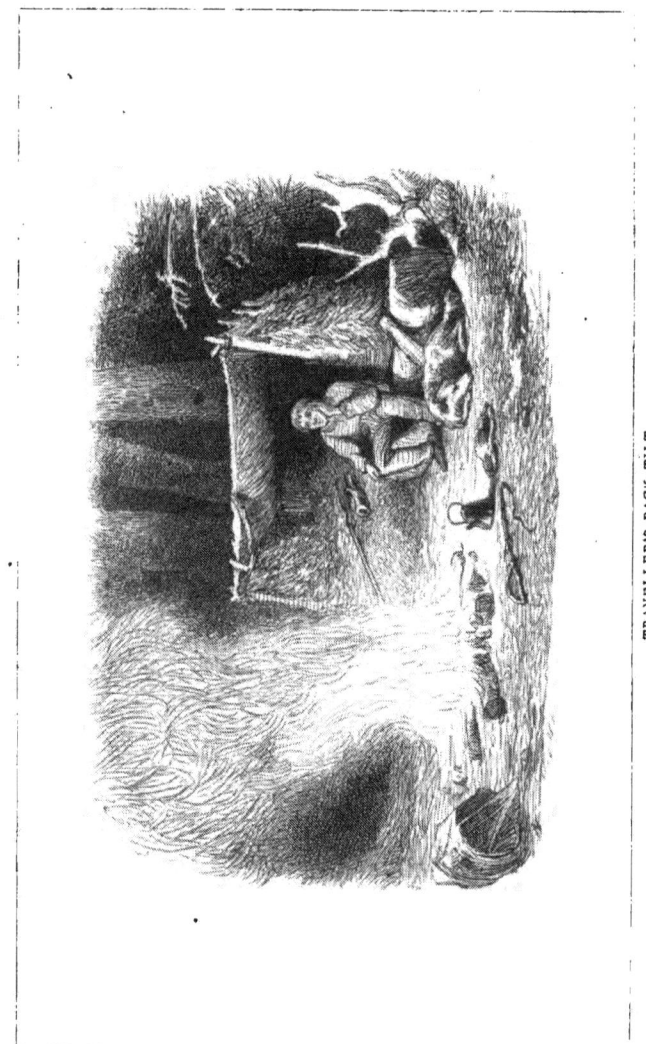

TRAVELLER'S BACK-TILT.

ling now become that we were nearly four hours getting over that short distance. The snow having concealed every thing upon the ground, we could not avoid the rivulets, and when we happened to step on the place underneath which one of them ran, the ice at once broke in, and we sank deep in snow and water.

A laughable adventure which I will here relate befell me near the end of my journey homewards. When I reached Locker's Bay several young men at that place were preparing to start for Greens-pond and join their vessels for the ice voyage, and they proposed to travel in company with me the next day. In the morning of our departure they determined to save time and toil, by first going a mile or so to a part of the shore where there was no ice, and launch a punt with sails. By this means we hoped to accomplish great part of the distance by water, and to rest at Fair Islands that night. At noon we had our punt under way, with two sails set, and a fine fair wind blowing fresh. The four oars were also put out to help our boat along. But the cold was extreme, and ice made upon the water so fast that in five hours we only proceeded four miles. It was then getting dark, and we consulted how to get shelter for the night. We were far from any woody land, but a high cliff

was under our lee, and a rocky shore beneath
the cliff. Here we determined to haul up our
punt, and turn it over so as to form a shelter for
us during the night. After we got ashore one
of our party remembered that an Irishman had
a tilt about a mile distant from us, but he supposed I would not like to take refuge there,
because the family were not members of my
flock[*]. Of course I overruled this objection,
and thither we went to ask for a lodging. We
found the tilt a very small one, and the family
which occupied it very large. There were the
father and mother, three stout adult sons, some
daughters, a woman servant, and a man of remarkable and very unprepossessing appearance,
whom they called "Uncle Billy." It was not
surprising that these many occupants of a little
house looked distressed at the intrusion of eight
men seeking quarters. They soon, however, made
my companions sufficiently welcome, seating them
round the fire and talking freely. Of me they
took no notice, and no place was left for me on
the bench and boxes which were the only seats.
Pressed by necessity, I determined to get a better
welcome, and tried to force myself upon these
people's notice by joining in their conversation.

* They were Roman Catholics.

This could not long continue without some remark on their part, so the master of the house
at length asked aloud of one of the company,
" Who is that man ?"   He was told, and then
he professed his pleasure in receiving me, and
sorrow that he could do so in no better style.
" Little did I think ever to have the honour of
receiving a jintleman like your riverence in this
poor place.   May be your riverence wouldn't
take a pipe ?"   I was not a habitual smoker,
but it seemed so sure a way to win the man's
heart that I at once said I would.   I had no
thought that one only pipe served the family,
or I would have refused the offer.   The man
asked his sons, " Boys, have yez a pipe ?"   They
sullenly answered, " No."   " Uncle Billy, have
ye e'er a one ?"   " I've no pipes," replied Uncle
Billy, very surlily, who seemed of the whole party
least inclined to like me.   The man then offered
me the little black dudeen which he was himself
smoking, and to avoid offence I used it for two
or three minutes with the best grace I could;
and now I was installed by the fire with every
mark of respect.   This family had been cruelly
robbed of the best articles of their winter's food
out of a little storehouse by the shore, and were
much straitened by their loss; but they gave me
the best supper they could, and were really kind.

By and by I heard a whispering about the minister's bed, and I protested at once against taking one, expressing my determination to lie by the fireside as I had already done for many nights. This could not be allowed, and Uncle Billy's bed was got ready for me. It was a cabin in a very small lean-to by the side of the house. In proper time I retired to the bed I had unwillingly accepted, and exhausted with the day's work soon sank to sleep between the blankets which seemed to have been in Uncle Billy's use without sheets for many months. Soon I was aroused by some one feeling about the foot of the bed, and looking up I recognized by the firelight, which shone into the little chamber, the head of Uncle Billy, and at once I guessed his purpose. He turned up the blankets, and got in at the foot of the bed he had plainly grudged to resign to me, and there he lay with his feet in most unpleasant nearness to my head. As soon as it was sufficiently broad day for me with decency to arise, I did so, and took my departure. I believe the master of the house did not know of Uncle Billy's intrusion, and would not have sanctioned it; but I am sorry to add, to the discredit of his hospitality, that he made me pay extravagantly for my night's lodging. Coming to me at my house in Greenspond

shortly afterwards, he borrowed of me, on pre-
text of the robbery he had suffered, the price of
a hundredweight of bread and several gallons of
molasses, and this he never attempted to repay,
though he had both opportunity and ability to
do so many times.

In all my journeyings through my mission, I
observed a rule suggested to me by a senior
brother missionary, in Newfoundland, at the
beginning of my work there: that in each place,
on each separate visit, I resorted for lodging and
refreshment to the same house which first received me. The only exception to this rule
would be, either in the case of my entertainers
proving of immoral and incorrigible character;
or of their becoming and declaring themselves
too poor to afford me any longer the temporary
maintenance. The former case, I am thankful
to say, never happened to me, and the latter
occurred but once.

It will probably be observed, by many readers,
that the missionary's possession of a boat is
essential to the proper service of such a mission
as I have now described. The expense of this
most valuable adjunct is however far beyond
his means. Besides the first cost, there must
be an annual outlay for the hire and maintenance

H

of a man servant, and for renewal and repair of the boat and her gear.

In concluding my account of the mode of serving my late mission, I may mention a practice which I ever found a means of winning the regard of my people, and which gave me many opportunities of profitable influence. It was the making myself composer and writer of letters for every one who chose to ask that service of me. This office often takes time that can very ill be spared from other business; but it is always worthy of ready attention. One person for whom a letter is written tells others, and they seek the same help when they have occasion for it, till at last the clergyman finds that he has incurred the care of keeping up a really large amount of correspondence. Many of my people had friends in England, with whom they regularly exchanged letters; and I was always asked to read those they received, and to reply to them. Very little of the contents of a letter will be dictated by the sender. Commonly he says, " O, sir, you know what to say much better than I can tell you." And so a clergyman really does know. He is acquainted with the state of each family; he knows the changes by sickness, death, or loss of property, which have affected them; he understands their hopes and fears for the future nearly as fully as they do, or at least as fully as they would care to make them known; and these things he can express in language more readily and better than they can, and he may always use the opportunity to add such reflections as are suitable and instructive both to the sender and receiver of the letter.

My little book must soon be closed. I will trespass no further now upon my reader's attention than to transcribe in conclusion the words of a venerable Bishop', now gone to his rest, to the accuracy and wisdom of whose remarks upon the Church's work in Newfoundland, I would humbly add such testimony as my experience in that work may have qualified me to give.

"There are peculiar circumstances at Newfoundland which increase the difficulties of providing for the instruction of the people. Their settlements are greatly scattered; always difficult of access, and often inaccessible. During the short fishing season every one is wholly engaged in the fishery, on which they depend

' See a letter of the late Bishop (Inglis) of Nova Scotia, in the Report of the Society for the Propagation of the Gospel, 1827-8.

for support; and in the winter it is a frequent practice to remove to the forest for shelter, fuel, and employment in preparing lumber. These difficulties however may be successfully met by becoming earnestness and zeal. Sometimes it will be desirable for the schoolmasters to move with the people, and tilt (as it is called) in the woods. The clergyman also must be ready, with a pure missionary spirit, to visit occasionally these temporary lodgments in the forest; and during the busiest seasons they will always find the general inclination of the people leaning towards the Church. Pressed as they often are by the hurry of the fishing season, they will always be ready for instruction, even then, on the Sabbath, which is seldom violated by Protestants here. But a personal intercourse must be kept up, through every difficulty, between the clergy and all the members of their flocks, or their influence will not be such as it ought to be.

"A missionary without missionary zeal can do nothing here. He will often have formidable difficulties to contend with; but if he be earnest in the great cause in which he is embarked, he will not be left without much comfort and encouragement in his arduous course. A large increase of the clergy and schoolmasters is immediately required, and under right direction, and with a blessing upon their labours, their services cannot fail to be of the highest value [8]. The means for defraying the necessary expense, would not long be withheld by those who have power to supply them, if they could witness the great spiritual wants, and the worthiness of the objects which require their benevolent regard and assistance."

Let me adopt as my own the final words of the good Bishop whom I have been citing:— "I have only to commend the whole work to the great Shepherd of the Christian Fold, and earnestly implore His blessing upon every endeavour to promote the salvation of His numerous flock."

[8] I feel certain that the whole of this and the succeeding sentence would be echoed by the present Bishop of Newfoundland, as strictly applicable to the circumstances of his diocese at this moment.

APPENDIX A.

(Page 61.)

It will interest many readers to know the cost of building and furnishing a substantial and sufficiently handsome wooden church in Newfoundland. The following account is a summary of the expense of the new church in Greenspond.

	£	s.	d.
Wages of carpenters and labourers . . .	430	17	7
Lumber	254	13	4
Nails, hinges, locks, and iron-work . . .	43	8	6
Paint, oil, putty, tar, and pitch . .	20	14	9
Windows	44	8	6
Bell (2 cwt.), with stock and wheel . . .	30	0	0
Altar-cloth	9	1	3
Carpets	18	0	0
Stoves	14	0	0
Books, holy table, chancel and font-rails, pulpit, prayer-desk, stove-funnels and fittings .	59	19	6
Newfoundland currency	£925	3	5
English money	£771	0	0

This summary, made before the accounts were finally closed, may be slightly in error, but is sufficiently correct for the present purpose. The flock contributed in money and money's worth about 750*l.*, and the remaining 175*l.* was given by the Bishop, the Diocesan Church Society, and other friends. The church will conveniently receive a congregation of 700 persons.

APPENDIX B.

(Page 62.)

I AM firmly convinced that this *must* be an exception to the case of the greater number of the missions in Newfoundland. Few places in that country are so prosperous as Greenspond long has been, chiefly by reason of its position. No other mission has so large a number of Church members. By my own two years' experience of another mission, and my full knowledge of one held by my late brother for six years, and by the testimony of several of my brother clergy respecting their flocks, it is to me certain that the Church of Newfoundland will ever need the

charitable aid of Churchmen at home.   At the
same time it may be truly said of most of these
people, that they do much, very much, for their
Church's maintenance.

. In my last mission, persons who had no food
but potatoes gave money to a fund for building a
parsonage, and some who through poverty were
drinking their tea without molasses, paid me
their year's dues.   The contribution was very
general, and in large proportion to the means of
most of the contributors, yet from a flock of
2700 Church members the dues paid did not
amount to 70*l*. currency, or 58*l*. English, and
from that sum 13*l*. had to be paid to readers.

APPENDIX C.

(Page 74.)

AFTER that sad " spring of the wrecks," a prayer,
which is an adaptation of one in the appointed
" Form of Prayers to be Used at Sea," was
printed and circulated throughout Greenspond
Mission with very happy effect.   In hope that

it may be further useful the prayer is here given :—

"*A Prayer for the use of Persons at Sea,*
Daily.

"O Eternal Lord God, Who alone spreadest out the heavens and rulest the raging of the sea; Who hast compassed the waters with bounds until day and night come to an end; be pleased to receive into Thy almighty and most gracious protection the persons of us Thy servants and the vessel in which we sail. Preserve us from the dangers of the sea, and grant us in peace and quietness to serve Thee our God, and that we may return in safety to enjoy the blessings of the land with the fruits of our labours, and with a thankful remembrance of Thy mercies to praise and glorify Thy holy Name, through Jesus Christ our Lord. Amen.

"Prevent us, O Lord, in all our doings," &c.

For the families on shore this was altered by changing the person and substituting for "us Thy servants," "all Thy servants engaged in the sealing voyage, especially A. B."

The sealing voyage, with its peculiar dangers, was a matter of such anxious concern to the whole flock, that few slighted prayer in this

I

behalf when they were guided to it. Persons who could not read learned it from those who could; and I remember especially one poor woman, whose life had been worse than careless, teaching her sick child to say this prayer in behalf of his absent father. It is obvious how great a step was thus gained towards forming the habit of prayer.

THE END.

GILBERT AND RIVINGTON, PRINTERS, ST. JOHN'S SQUARE, LONDON.

BOOKS LATELY PUBLISHED.

JOURNAL of a TOUR in ITALY: with Reflections on the Present Condition and Prospects of Religion in that Country. By CHR. WORDSWORTH, D.D., Canon of Westminster. 2 vols. post 8vo. 15s.

EIGHTEEN YEARS of a CLERICAL MEETING: being the Minutes of the Alcester Clerical Association, from 1842 to 1860; with a Preface on the Revival of Ruridecanal Chapters. Edited by RICHARD SEYMOUR, M.A., Rector of Kinwarton and Rural Dean; and JOHN F. MACKARNESS, M.A., late Vicar of Tardebigge, in the Diocese of Worcester, now Rector of Honiton. Crown 8vo. 6s. 6d.

An EXAMINATION of BISHOP COLENSO'S DIFFI-CULTIES with regard to the Pentateuch. By the Rev. ALEX-ANDER McCAUL, D.D., Professor of Hebrew and Old Testament Exegesis, King's College, London. *Second Library Edition.* Crown 8vo. 5s.

Also, The PEOPLE'S EDITION of the above Work. *Sixth Thousand.* 1s.

The MAN CHRIST JESUS; or, The Daily Life, and Teaching of our Lord, in Childhood and Manhood, on Earth. By the Rev. THOMAS MARKBY, M.A., lately Afternoon Lecturer at St. James's, Paddington. Crown 8vo. 9s. 6d.

LAMPS of the CHURCH; or, Rays of Faith, Hope, and Charity, from the Lives and Deaths of some eminent Christians of the Nineteenth Century. By the Rev. H. CLISSOLD, M.A., Author of "Last Hours of Eminent Christians." Crown 8vo., *with five Portraits beautifully engraved on Steel.* 9s. 6d.

BRIEF MEMORIALS of the late Rev. CHARLES GREEN, M.A., of Worcester College, Oxford; Missionary and Secretary of the Society for the Propagation of the Gospel. Small 8vo. 2s. 6d.

FEBRUARY, 1863.

A

SELECT LIST OF WORKS

PUBLISHED BY

MESSRS. RIVINGTON,

3, WATERLOO PLACE, PALL MALL, LONDON.

Adams's (Rev. W.) The Shadow of the Cross ; an Allegory.
A New Edition, elegantly printed in crown 8vo., with Illustrations.
3s. 6d. in extra cloth, gilt edges.

———— The Distant Hills ; an Allegory. New Edition.
Small 8vo. 2s. 6d. .

———— The Old Man's Home ; a Tale. New Edition.
Small 8vo. 2s. 6d.

———— The King's Messengers ; an Allegorical Tale. New
Edition. Small 8vo. 2s. 6d.

———— Cheap Editions of the Four Allegories, for distribution, 1s. each.

———— A Collected Edition of the Four Allegories, with
Memoir and Portrait of the Author: elegantly printed in crown 8vo. 9s.
cloth, or 14s. in morocco.

———— An Illustrated Edition of the above Sacred Allegories, with numerous Engravings on Wood from Original Designs by
C. W. Cope, R.A., J. C. Horsley, A.R.A., Samuel Palmer, Birket
Forster, and George E. Hicks. Small 4to. 21s. in extra cloth, or 36s. in
antique morocco.

———— The Warnings of the Holy Week ; being a Course
of Parochial Lectures for the Week before Easter, and the Easter Festivals.
Fifth Edition. Small 8vo. 4s. 6d.

A

Alford's (Dean) Greek Testament; with a critically revised
Text: a Digest of Various Readings: Marginal References to Verbal and
Idiomatic Usage: Prolegomena: and a copious Critical and Exegetical
Commentary in English. In 4 vols. 8vo. 5l. 2s.

Or, separately,

Vol. I.—The Four Gospels. Fourth Edition. 28s.
Vol. II.—Acts to II. Corinthians. Fourth Edition. 24s.
Vol. III.—Galatians to Philemon. Third Edition. 18s.
Vol. IV.—Hebrews to Revelation. Second Edition. 32s.
The Fourth Volume may still be had in Two Parts.

—— **Sermons on Christian Doctrine, preached in Canter-**
bury Cathedral, on the Afternoons of the Sundays in the year 1861-62.
Crown 8vo. 7s. 6d.

—— **Sermons preached at Quebec Chapel, 1854 to 1857.**
In Seven Volumes, small 8vo. 2l. 1s.

Sold separately as follows:—

Vols. I. and II. (A course for the Year.) Second Edition. 12s. 6d.
Vol. III. (On Practical Subjects.) 7s. 6d.
Vol. IV. (On Divine Love.) Second Edition. 5s.
Vol. V. (On Christian Practice.) Second Edition. 5s.
Vol. VI. (On the Person and Office of Christ.) 5s.
Vol. VII. (Concluding Series.) 6s.

—— **Homilies on the Former Part of the Acts of the**
Apostles (Chap. I.—X.); delivered at Quebec Chapel. 8vo. 8s.

—— **Poetical Works. Third Edition. Crown 8vo. 8s. 6d.**

American Church.—Recent Recollections of the Anglo-
American Church in the United States. By an English Layman, five
years resident in that Republic. 2 vols. post 8vo. 18s.

Anderson's (Hon. Mrs.) Practical Religion exemplified, by
Letters and Passages from the Life of the late Rev. Robert Anderson, of
Brighton. Sixth Edition. Small 8vo. 4s.

Anderson's (Rev. J. S. M.) History of the Church of Eng-
land in the Colonies and Foreign Dependencies of the British Empire.
Second Edition. In 3 vols. small 8vo. 24s.

—— **Addresses, chiefly to Young Men. Contents:—1. On**
the Profitable Employment of Hours gained from Business. 2. Dr.
Johnson. 3. Columbus. 4. Sir Walter Raleigh. 5. England and her
Colonies. Second Edition. Small 8vo. 4s. 6d.

Annual Register; or, a View of History and Politics for
each year; with a Chronicle of Events; Public Documents; Remarkable Law Cases; Honours and Promotions; Births, Deaths, and Marriages,
&c. &c.: the whole forming a Volume of about 850 pages, published
annually about Midsummer, price 18s.
No library can be complete without this important Series.

Arnold's (Rev. T. K.) School-books (see page 18).

Arnold's (Rev. T. K.) Sermons preached in a Country Village. Post 8vo. 5s. 6d.

Arnold's (Rev. Dr. T.) History of Rome, from the Earliest Period to the End of the Second Punic War. New Edition. 3 vols. 8vo. 36s.

———————————— History of the later Roman Commonwealth, from the End of the Second Punic War to the Death of Julius Cæsar, with the Reign of Augustus, and a Life of Trajan. New Edition. 2 vols. 8vo. 24s.

Aspinall's (Rev. James) Parish Sermons, as preached from his own Pulpit. In 2 vols. small 8vo. 5s. each.

Atkins's (Rev. Dr.) Six Discourses on Pastoral Duties, preached before the University of Dublin; being the Donnellan Lectures for 1860. 8vo. 6s.

Barrow's (Dr. Isaac) Works; compared with the Original MSS. and enlarged with Materials hitherto unpublished. A New Edition, by A. Napier, M.A., of Trinity College, Vicar of Holkham, Norfolk. 9 vols. 8vo. 4l. 14s. 6d.

Bean's (Rev. James) Family Worship; a Course of Morning and Evening Prayers for every Day in the Month. Twentieth Edition. Small 8vo. 4s. 6d.

Beaven's (Rev. Dr.) Help to Catechising; for the use of Clergymen, Schools, and Private Families. New Edition. 18mo. 2s.

Berens's (Archdeacon) Thirty-three Village Sermons, on the chief Articles of Faith, and the Means of Grace, on certain Parts of the Christian Character, and on some of the Relative Duties. New Edition. 12mo. 4s. 6d.

———————————— Twenty-six Village Sermons. Second Edition. 12mo. 5s. 6d.

———————————— Selection from the Papers of Addison in the Spectator and Guardian; for the Use of Young Persons. New Edition. 12mo. 4s. 6d.

———————————— Christmas Stories. Contents:—Good Nature — The Smuggler — Village Politics — and Robin Goodfellow. Seventh Edition. Small 8vo. 3s.

Bethell's (late Bp. of Bangor) General View of the Doctrine of Regeneration in Baptism. Fifth Edition. 8vo. 9s.

Bickersteth's (Archdeacon) Questions illustrating the Thirty-nine Articles of the Church of England: with Proofs from Scripture and the Primitive Church. Fourth Edition. 12mo. 3s. 6d.

———————————— Catechetical Exercises on the Apostles' Creed; chiefly drawn from the Exposition of Bishop Pearson. New Edition. 18mo. 2s.

A 2

Bray's (Rev. E. A.) Sermons, General and Occasional. 2 vols. small 8vo. 14s.

Burke.—A Complete Edition of the Works and Correspondence of the Right Hon. Edmund Burke. In 8 vols. 8vo. *With Portrait. 4l. 4s.*

     Contents :—1. Mr. Burke's Correspondence between the year 1744 and his Decease in 1797, first published from the original MSS. in 1844, edited by Earl Fitzwilliam and Sir Richard Bourke. The most interesting portion of the Letters of Mr. Burke to Dr. French Laurence is also included in it.

     2. The Works of Mr. Burke, as edited by his Literary Executors, and completed by the publication of the 15th and 16th Volumes, in 1826, under the Superintendence of the late Bishop of Rochester, Dr. Walker King.

Burke's (Edmund) Reflections on the Revolution in France, in 1790. New Edition, with a short Biographical Notice. 8vo. 4s. 6d.

Byng's (Rev. F. E. C.) Sermons for Households. Crown 8vo. 3s. 6d.

Caswall's (Rev. Dr.) Martyr of the Pongas. A Memoir of the Rev. Hamble James Leacock, first West-Indian Missionary to Western Africa. Small 8vo. With Portrait. 5s. 6d.

———————————— The Prophet of the Nineteenth Century ; or, the Rise, Progress, and Present State (1843) of the Mormons, or, Latter-Day Saints. To which is appended, an Analysis of the Book of Mormon. Post 8vo. 7s. 6d.

Chevallier's (Rev. Professor) Translation of the Epistles of Clemens Romanus, Ignatius, and Polycarp, and of the Apologies of Justin Martyr and Tertullian. With Notes, and an Account of the Present State of the Question respecting the Epistles of Ignatius. Second Edition. 8vo. 12s.

Christian's (The) Duty, from the Sacred Scriptures. In Two Parts. Part I. Exhortation to Repentance and a Holy Life. Part II. Devotions for the Closet, in Three Offices, for every Day in the Week. [*London : sold by C. Rivington, in St. Paul's Churchyard.* 1730.] New Edition. Edited by the Rev. Thomas Dale, M.A. Small 8vo. (1852.) 5s.

Clabon's (John M.) Praise, Precept, and Prayer ; a Complete Manual of Family Worship. Part I. From the Old Testament, for Morning use. Part II. From the Old and New Testaments, and from the best Commentators, for Evening use. Part III. From " The Imitation of Christ." Part IV. Prayers for Six Weeks. 8vo. 16s.

Clergy Charities.—List of Charities, General and Diocesan, for the Relief of the Clergy, their Widows and Families. Third Edition. Small 8vo. 3s.

Clissold's (Rev. H.) Lamps of the Church; or, Rays of Faith, Hope, and Charity, from the Lives and Deaths of some Eminent Christians of the Nineteenth Century. Crown 8vo., *with five Portraits on Steel*, 9s. 6d. *In morocco*, 15s.

Cottager's Monthly Visitor.—Thirty-six Volumes of this Work have been published, forming a Repository of Religious Instruction and Domestic Economy, suited to Family Reading, the Parochial Library, and the Servants' Hall. Its contents include Spiritual Exposition, Instructive Tales, Hints on Gardening and Agriculture, and short Extracts from the best Authors. All the volumes are sold separately, 4s. *each*.

Cotterill's Selection of Psalms and Hymns for Public Worship. New and cheaper Editions. 32mo., 1s.; in 18mo. (large print), 1s. 6d. Also an Edition on fine paper, 2s. 6d.

*** A large allowance to Clergymen and Churchwardens.

Cureton's (Rev. Dr.) Corpus Ignatianum; or, a Complete Body of the Ignatian Epistles: Genuine, Interpolated, and Spurious, according to the three Recensions. With numerous extracts, in Syriac, Greek, and Latin, and an English Translation of the Syrian Text; an Introduction, and copious Notes. Royal 8vo. 31s. 6d.

——————————— Spicilegium Syriacum; or, Remnants of Writers of the Second and Third Centuries, preserved in Syriac, with an English Translation, and Notes. Royal 8vo. 9s.

Davys's (Bp. of Peterborough) Plain and Short History of England for Children: in Letters from a Father to his Son. With Questions. Thirteenth Edition. 18mo. 2s. 6d.

——————————— Volume for a Lending Library; chiefly selected from the *Cottager's Monthly Visitor*. Small 8vo. 4s. 6d.

Early Influences. By the Author of "Truth without Prejudice." Third Edition. Small 8vo. 3s. 6d.

Ellison's (Rev. H. J.) Way of Holiness in Married Life; a Course of Sermons preached in Lent. Second Edition. Small 8vo. 2s. 6d. *In white cloth, antique style*, 3s. 6d.

Elsley's Annotations on the Four Gospels, and the Acts of the Apostles. Compiled and abridged for the Use of Students. Eighth Edition. 2 vols. 8vo. 16s.

Evans's (Archdeacon) Scripture Biography. In 3 vols. small 8vo. 18s.

——————————— Biography of the Early Church. Second Edition. 2 vols. small 8vo. 12s.

——————————— Bishopric of Souls. Fourth Edition. Small 8vo. 5s.

Evans's (Archdeacon) Ministry of the Body. Second Edition. Small 8vo. 6s. 6d.

Euripidis Tragœdiæ Priores Quatuor. Edidit Ricardus Porson, A.M. Recensuit suasque Notulas subjecit Jacobus Scholefield, A.M. Third Edition. 8vo. 10s. 6d.

Exton's (Rev. R. B.) Speculum Gregis; or, the Parochial Minister's Assistant in the Oversight of his Flock. With blank forms to be filled up at discretion. Seventh Edition. In pocket size. 4s. 6d. bound with clasp.

Fearon's (Rev. H.) Sermons on Public Subjects. Small 8vo. 3s. 6d.

Frampton's (Miss) Short Account of the Lives and Martyrdom of the Apostles, Evangelists, Disciples, and Earliest Fathers of the Church who suffered for the truth of Christianity. Small 8vo. 2s. 6d.

Galloway's (Rev. W. B.) Clergyman's Holidays: or, Friendly Discussions, Historical, Scriptural, and Philosophical. Small 8vo. 5s.

———————————— Ezekiel's Sign, Metrically Paraphrased and Interpreted, from his Fourth and Fifth Chapters; with Notes, and Elucidations from the Sculptured Slabs of Nineveh. Small 8vo. 2s. 6d.

Gilly's (late Canon) Memoir of Felix Neff, Pastor of the High Alps; and of his Labours among the French Protestants of Dauphiné, a Remnant of the Primitive Christians of Gaul. Sixth Edition. Fcap. 5s. 6d.

Girdlestone's (Rev. Charles) Holy Bible, containing the Old and New Testaments; with a Commentary arranged in Short Lectures for the Daily Use of Families. New Edition, in 6 vols. 8vo. 3l. 3s.

The Old Testament separately. 4 vols. 8vo. 42s.
The New Testament. 2 vols. 8vo. 21s.

Goulburn's (Rev. Dr.) Thoughts on Personal Religion. Third Edition. Small 8vo. 6s. 6d.

———————————— Sermons preached on Various Occasions during the last Twenty Years. In 2 vols. small 8vo. 10s. 6d.

———————————— Introduction to the Devotional Study of the Holy Scriptures. Fifth Edition. Small 8vo. 4s. 6d.

Gray's (late Bp. of Bristol) Key to the Old Testament and Apocrypha: or, an Account of their several Books, of the Contents and Authors, and of the Times in which they were respectively written. Tenth Edition. 8vo. 10s. 6d.

Green.—Brief Memorials of the late Rev. Charles Green, M.A., of Worcester College, Oxford; Missionary and Secretary of the Society for the Propagation of the Gospel. Small 8vo. 2s. 6d.

Greswell's (Rev. Edward) The Three Witnesses and the Threefold Cord; being the Testimony of the Natural Measures of Time, of the Primitive Civil Calendar, and of Antediluvian and Postdiluvian Tradition, on the Principal Questions of Fact in Sacred or Profane Antiquity. 8vo. 7s. 6d.

———————————————————— Exposition of the Parables and of other Parts of the Gospels. 5 vols. (in 6 parts), 8vo. 3l. 12s.

Grotius de Veritate Religionis Christianæ. With English Notes and Illustrations, for the use of Students. By the Rev. J. E. Middleton, M.A., of Trinity College, Cambridge; Lecturer on Theology at St. Bees' College. Second Edition. 12mo. 6s.

Gurney's (Rev. J. H.) Sermons on the Acts of the Apostles. Small 8vo. 7s.

———————————————————— Sermons chiefly on Old Testament Histories, from Texts in the Sunday Lessons. Second Edition. 6s.

———————————————————— Sermons on Texts from the Epistles and Gospels for Twenty Sundays. Second Edition. 6s.

———————————————————— Miscellaneous Sermons. 6s.

Hale's (Archdeacon) Sick Man's Guide to Acts of Faith, Patience, Charity, and Repentance. Extracted from Bishop Taylor's Holy Dying. In large print. Second Edition. 8vo. 3s.

Hall's (Rev. W. J.) Psalms and Hymns adapted to the Services of the Church of England. In 8vo., 8s.—18mo., 3s.—24mo., 1s. 6d.—24mo., limp cloth, 1s. 3d.—24mo., fine paper, 2s.—32mo., 1s.—32mo., limp, 8d.—32mo., fine paper, 2s.

———————————————————— Selection of Tunes. Royal 8vo., 12s. Oblong 12mo., 3s. 6d.

₊ A Prospectus of the above, with Specimens of Type, and farther particulars, may be had of the Publishers.

Hannah's (Rev. Dr.) Discourses on the Fall and its Results. Small 8vo. 5s.

Harcourt's (Rev. L. Vernon) New Harmony of the Gospels, in the Form of Lectures. In 3 vols. 8vo. 2l. 8s.

Hawkins's (Rev. W. B.) Limits of Religious Belief: Suggestions addressed to the Student in Divine Things. Small 8vo. 2s. 6d.

Help and Comfort for the Sick Poor. By the Author of "Sickness: its Trials and Blessings." Fourth Edition, in large print. 1s., or 1s. 6d. in cloth.

Henley's (Hon. and Rev. R.) The Prayer of Prayers. Small 8vo. 4s. 6d.

Hey's (John) Lectures on Divinity, delivered in the University of Cambridge. Third Edition, by T. Turton, D.D., Lord Bishop of Ely. 2 vols. 8vo. 30s.

Heygate's (Rev. W. E.) Care of the Soul; or, Sermons on Points of Christian Prudence. 12mo. 5s. 6d.

———————— The Good Shepherd; or, Christ the Pattern, Priest, and Pastor. 18mo. 3s. 6d.

Hodgson's (Chr.) Instructions for the Use of Candidates for Holy Orders, and of the Parochial Clergy, as to Ordination, Licences, Induction, Pluralities, Residence, &c. &c.; with Acts of Parliament relating to the above, and Forms to be used. Eighth Edition. 8vo. 12s.

  ₊ In this Edition such alterations have been made as appeared to be necessary in consequence of recent amendments in the laws relating to the Clergy.

Holden's (Rev. Geo.) Christian Expositor; or, Practical Guide to the Study of the New Testament. Intended for the use of General Readers. Second Edition. 12mo. 12s.

Holy Thoughts; or, A Treasury of True Riches. Collected chiefly from our Old Writers. Eighth Edition. 1s. 6d.

Homilies (The) with Various Readings, and the Quotations from the Fathers given at length in the Original Languages. Edited by G. E. Corrie, D.D. 8vo. 10s. 6d.

Hook's (Dean) Book of Family Prayer. Sixth Edition. 18mo. 2s.

—————— Private Prayers. Fifth Edition. 18mo. 2s.

—————— Dictionary of Ecclesiastical Biography. 8 vols. 12mo. 2l. 11s.

Hooper's (Rev. F. B.) Exposition of the Revelations. 2 vols. 8vo. 28s.

Hulton's (Rev. C. G.) Catechetical Help to Bishop Butler's Analogy. Third Edition. Post 8vo. 4s. 6d.

Hymns and Poems for the Sick and Suffering; in connexion with the Service for the Visitation of the Sick. Selected from various Authors. Edited by the Rev. T. V. Fosbery, M.A., Vicar of St. Giles's, Reading. Fifth Edition. 5s. 6d. in cloth, or 9s. 6d. in morocco.

  This Volume contains 233 separate pieces; of which about 90 are by writers who lived prior to the 18th Century; the rest are modern, and some of these original. Amongst the names of the writers (between 70 and 80 in number) occur those of Sir J. Beaumont—Sir T. Browne—Elizabeth of Bohemia—Phineas Fletcher—George Herbert—Dean Hickes—Bp. Ken—Quarles—Sandys—Jeremy Taylor—Henry Vaughan—and Sir H. Wotton. And of modern writers—Mrs. Barrett Browning—Bishop Wilberforce—S. T. Coleridge—W. Wordsworth—Dean Trench—Rev. Messrs. Chandler—Keble—Lyte—Monsell and Moultrie.

Jackson's (Bp. of Lincoln) Six Sermons on the Christian Character; preached in Lent. Seventh Edition. Small 8vo. 3s. 6d.

James's (Rev. Dr.) Comment upon the Collects appointed to be used in the Church of England on Sundays and Holydays throughout the Year. Fifteenth Edition. 12mo. 5s.

——————————— Christian Watchfulness in the Prospect of Sickness, Mourning, and Death. Eighth Edition. 12mo. 6s.

Cheap Editions of these two works may be had, price 3s. each.

——————————— Evangelical Life, as seen in the Example of our Lord Jesus Christ. Second Edition. 12mo. 7s. 6d.

——————————— Devotional Comment on the Morning and Evening Services in the Book of Common Prayer, in a Series of Plain Lectures. Second Edition. In 2 vols. 12mo. 10s. 6d.

Inman's (Rev. Professor) Treatise on Navigation and Nautical Astronomy, for the Use of British Seamen. Thirteenth Edition, edited by the Rev. J. W. Inman. Royal 8vo. 7s.

——————————— Nautical Tables for the Use of British Seamen. New Edition, edited by the Rev. J. W. Inman. Royal 8vo. 14s.

Kaye's (late Bp. of Lincoln) Account of the Writings and Opinions of Justin Martyr. Third Edition. 8vo. 7s. 6d.

——————————— Ecclesiastical History of the Second and Third Centuries, Illustrated from the Writings of Tertullian. Third Edition. 8vo. 13s.

——————————— Account of the Writings and Opinions of Clement of Alexandria. 8vo. 12s.

——————————— Account of the Council of Nicæa, in connexion with the Life of Athanasius. 8vo. 8s.

Kennaway's (Rev. C. E.) Consolatio; or, Comfort for the Afflicted. Selected from various Authors. With a Preface by the Bishop of Oxford. Tenth Edition. Small 8vo. 4s. 6d.

Landon's (Rev. E. H.) Manual of Councils of the Holy Catholic Church, comprising the Substance of the most Remarkable and Important Canons. Alphabetically arranged. 12mo. 12s.

Latin Reader.—De Viris Illustribus Urbis Romæ, a Romulo ad Augustum. An Elementary Latin Reading Book, being a Series of Biographical Chapters on Roman History, chronologically arranged. By the Editor of the "Graduated Series of English Reading Books." Small 8vo. 3s.

Lee's (Rev. Professor) Inspiration of Holy Scripture, its Nature and Proof: Eight Discourses preached before the University of Dublin. Second Edition, revised, with Index. 8vo. 14s.

Low (Bishop).—A Memoir of the Right Rev. David Low, D.D., formerly Bishop of the United Dioceses of Ross, Moray, and Argyle; comprising Sketches of the Principal Events connected with the Scottish Episcopal Church, during the last Seventy Years. By the Rev. William Blatch, Incumbent of St John's, Pittenweem, and late Clerical Assistant to the Bishop. 12mo. 7s.

Lyttelton's (Lord) Four Gospels and the Acts of the Apo- stles; with Explanatory Notes. Post 8vo. 4s. 6d.

McCaul's (Rev. Dr.) Testimonies to the Divine Authority and Inspiration of Holy Scripture, as taught by the Church of England. Crown 8vo. 4s. 6d.

—————————— **Examination of Bp. Colenso's Diffi-** culties with regard to the Pentateuch; and some Reasons for believing in its Authenticity and Divine Origin. Crown 8vo. 5s.

Mackenzie's (Rev. H.) Ordination Lectures, delivered in Riseholme Palace Chapel, during Ember Weeks. Small 8vo. 3s.

Contents:—Pastoral Government—Educational Work—Self-govern-ment in the Pastor—Missions and their Reflex Results—Dissent—Public Teaching—Sunday Schools—Doctrinal Controversy—Secular Aids.

Maitland's (Rev. Dr.) Voluntary System; in a Series of Letters. 12mo. 6s. 6d.

—————————— **Dark Ages: a Series of Essays in** illustration of the Religion and Literature of the Ninth, Tenth, Eleventh, and Twelfth Centuries. Third Edition. 8vo. 12s.

—————————— **Essays on Subjects connected with** the Reformation in England. 8vo. 15s.

Mant's (late Bishop) Book of Common Prayer and Adminis- tration of the Sacraments, with copious Notes, Practical and Historical, from approved Writers of the Church of England; including the Canons and Constitutions of the Church. New Edition. In one volume, super-royal 8vo. 24s.

—————————— **Happiness of the Blessed considered as to** the Particulars of their State; their Recognition of each other in that State; and its Difference of Degrees. Seventh Edition. 12mo. 4s.

Marsh's (late Bp. of Peterborough) Comparative View of the Churches of England and Rome: with an Appendix on Church Authority, the Character of Schism, and the Rock on which our Saviour declared that He would build His Church. Third Edition. Small 8vo. 6s.

Melvill's (Rev. H.) Sermons. Vol. I., Sixth Edition. Vol. II., Fourth Edition. 10s. 6d. each.

—————————— **Sermons on some of the less prominent** Facts and References in Sacred Story. Second Edition. 2 vols. 8vo. 10s. 6d. each.

Melvill's (Rev. H.) Selection from the Lectures delivered at St. Margaret's, Lothbury, on the Tuesday Mornings in the Years 1850, 1851, 1852. Small 8vo. 6s.

Middleton's (Bp.) Doctrine of the Greek Article applied to the Criticism and Illustration of the New Testament. By the late Bishop Middleton. With Prefatory Observations and Notes, by Hugh James Rose, B.D., late Principal of King's College, London. New Edition. In 8vo. 12s.

Mill's (Rev. Dr.) Analysis of Bishop Pearson on the Creed. Third Edition. 8vo. 5s.

Monsell's (Rev. Dr.) Parish Musings; or, Devotional Poems. Fifth Edition. 18mo. 2s.

Nixon's (Bp. of Tasmania) Lectures, Historical, Doctrinal, and Practical, on the Catechism of the Church of England. Sixth Edition. 8vo. 18s.

O'Keeffe's (Miss) Patriarchal Times; or, The Land of Canaan: in Seven Books. Comprising interesting Events, Incidents, and Characters, founded on the Holy Scriptures. Seventh Edition. Small 8vo. 6s. 6d.

Old Man's (The) Rambles. Sixth and cheaper Edition. 18mo. 3s. 6d.

Palmer's (Rev. W.) Origines Liturgicæ; or, the Antiquities of the English Ritual: with a Dissertation on Primitive Liturgies. Fourth Edition, enlarged. 2 vols. 8vo. 18s.

Parkinson's (Canon) Old Church Clock. Fourth Edition. Small 8vo. 4s. 6d.

Parry's (Mrs.) Young Christian's Sunday Evening; or, Conversations on Scripture History. In 3 vols. small 8vo. Sold separately:
First Series: on the Old Testament. Fourth Edition. 6s. 6d.
Second Series: on the Gospels. Third Edition. 7s.
Third Series: on the Acts. Second Edition. 4s. 6d.

Pearson's Exposition of the Creed; edited by Temple Chevallier, B.D., Professor of Mathematics in the University of Durham, and late Fellow and Tutor of St. Catharine's College, Cambridge. Second Edition. 8vo. 10s. 6d.

Peile's (Rev. Dr.) Annotations on the Apostolical Epistles. New Edition. 4 vols. 8vo. 42s.

Penny Sunday Reader.—This Work, first published in Numbers, consists of 14 volumes (sold separately, price 2s. 9d. each), and contains a plain, popular, and copious Commentary on the Book of Common Prayer; besides numerous Devotional Essays, Sacred Poetry, and Extracts from Eminent Divines. The earlier volumes were edited by the Rev. Dr. Molesworth, Vicar of Rochdale, and the whole Series is included in the List of Books recommended by the Society for Promoting Christian Knowledge.

Pepys's (Lady C.) Quiet Moments: a Four Weeks' Course of Thoughts and Meditations before Evening Prayer and at Sunset. Fourth Edition. Small 8vo. 3s. 6d.

———————— Morning Notes of Praise: a Companion Volume. Second Edition. 3s. 6d.

Pinder's (Rev. J. H.) Sermons on the Book of Common Prayer and Administration of the Sacraments. To which are now added, Several Sermons on the Feasts and Fasts of the Church, preached in the Cathedral Church of Wells. Third Edition. 12mo. 7s.

———————— Sermons on the Holy Days observed in the Church of England throughout the Year. Second Edition. 12mo. 6s. 6d.

———————— Meditations and Prayers on the Ordination Service for Deacons. Small 8vo. 3s. 6d.

———————— Meditations and Prayers on the Ordination Service for Priests. Small 8vo. 3s. 6d.

Plain Sermons. By Contributors to the "Tracts for the Times." In 10 vols. 8vo., 6s. 6d. each. (Sold separately.)

This Series contains 347 original Sermons of moderate length, written in simple language, and in an earnest and impressive style, forming a copious body of practical Theology, in accordance with the Doctrines of the Church of England. They are particularly suited for family reading. The last Volume contains a general Index of Subjects, and a Table of the Sermons adapted to the various Seasons of the Christian Year.

The Editor of the "Guardian," in a review of this Work, writes, "It is most interesting to learn that they are as popular in our Sister Church in America as in our own; and (a fact not a little remarkable) even among the Dissenters there, on account of that practical seriousness and reality which pervades them."

Prayers for the Sick and Dying. By the Author of "Sick-ness, its Trials and Blessings." Third Edition. Small 8vo. 2s. 6d.

Ramsay's (Dean) Catechism compiled and arranged for the use of Young Persons. Eighth Edition. 18mo. cloth, 2s. Or in limp cloth, 1s. 6d.

Reminiscences by a Clergyman's Wife. Edited by the Dean of Canterbury. Second Edition. Crown 8vo. 3s. 6d.

Schmitz's (Dr. L.) Manual of Ancient History, from the Remotest Times to the Overthrow of the Western Empire, A.D. 476. Third Edition. Crown 8vo. 7s. 6d.

This Work, for the convenience of Schools, may be had in Two Parts, sold separately, viz.:—

Vol. I., containing, besides the History of India and the other Asiatic Nations, a complete History of Greece. 4s.
Vol. II., containing a complete History of Rome. 4s.

Schmitz's (Dr. L.) Manual of Ancient Geography. Crown
8vo. 6s.

——————————— History of the Middle Ages. In 2
vols. Vol. I. (from the Downfall of the Western Empire, A.D. 476, to
the Crusades, A.D. 1096.) Crown 8vo. 7s. 6d.

Seymour's (Rev. R.) and Mackarness's (Rev. J. F.) Eighteen
Years of a Clerical Meeting : being the Minutes of the Alcester Clerical
Association, from 1842 to 1860 ; with a Preface on the Revival of Ruri-
decanal Chapters. Crown 8vo. 6s. 6d.

Shuttleworth's (late Bp. of Chichester) Paraphrastic Translation of the Apostolical Epistles, with Notes. Fifth Edition. 8vo. 9s.

Sickness, its Trials and Blessings. Seventh Edition. Small
8vo. 5s. Also, a cheaper Edition, for distribution, 2s. 6d.

Slade's (late Canon) Annotations on the Epistles ; being a
Continuation of Mr. Elsley's " Annotations on the Four Gospels and Acts
of the Apostles." Fifth Edition. 2 vols. 8vo. 18s.

——————————— Twenty-one Prayers composed from
the Psalms for the Sick and Afflicted : with other Forms of Prayer, and
Hints and Directions for the Visitation of the Sick. Seventh Edition.
12mo. 3s. 6d.

——————————— Plain Parochial Sermons. 7 vols. 12mo.
6s. each. (Sold separately.)

Smith's (John) Select Discourses. Edited by H. G. Williams, B.D., Professor of Arabic in the University of Cambridge.
Royal 8vo. 10s. 6d.

Smith's (Rev. Dr. J. B.) Manual of the Rudiments of
Theology : containing an Abridgment of Tomline's Elements ; an Analysis
of Paley's Evidences ; a Summary of Pearson on the Creed ; and a brief
Exposition of the Thirty-nine Articles, chiefly from Burnet ; Explanation
of Jewish Rites and Ceremonies, &c. &c. Fifth Edition. 12mo. 8s. 6d.

——————————— Compendium of Rudiments in
Theology : containing a Digest of Bishop Butler's Analogy ; an Epitome
of Dean Graves on the Pentateuch ; and an Analysis of Bishop Newton
on the Prophecies. Second Edition. 12mo. 9s.

——————————— Digest of Hooker's Treatise on
the Laws of Ecclesiastical Polity. For the use of Students. 12mo. 9s.

Sneyd's (Miss C. A.) Meditations for a Month, on Select
Passages of Scripture. Small 8vo. 3s. 6d.

Talbot's (Hon. Mrs. J. C.) Parochial Mission-Women ; their
Work and its Fruits. Second Edition. Small 8vo. In limp cloth, 2s.

The object of this little book is to give a sketch of a work which has now
for two years been carried on among the lowest classes of the population of
London and some other great towns, under the direct control of the
Parochial Clergy, and which appears to have succeeded in a remarkable
manner.

Threshold (The) of Private Devotion. 18mo. 2s.

Townsend's (Canon) Holy Bible, containing the Old and New Testaments, arranged in Historical and Chronological Order, so that the whole may be read as one connected History, in the words of the Authorized Translation. With copious Notes and Indexes. Fifth Edition. In 2 vols., imperial 8vo., 21s. each (sold separately).

Also, an Edition of this Arrangement of the Bible without the Notes, in One Volume, 14s.

——————————— Scriptural Communion with God; or, the Pentateuch and the Book of Job, arranged in Historical and Chronological Order, and newly divided into sections for daily reading; with Introductions and Prayers, and Notes for the Student and Inquirer. In 2 large vols. 8vo. 45s.

Trimmer's (the late Mrs.) Abridgment of Scripture History; consisting of Lessons from the Old Testament. New Edition. 12mo. 1s. 6d.

——————————— Abridgment of the New Testament; consisting of Lessons from the Writings of the Four Evangelists. New Edition. 12mo. 1s. 4d.

——————————— Help to the Unlearned in the Study of the Holy Scriptures. New Edition. 2 vols. 12mo. 10s.

Trollope's (Rev. W.) Iliad of Homer from a carefully corrected Text; with copious English Notes, illustrating the Grammatical Construction, the Manners and Customs, the Mythology and Antiquities of the Heroic Ages; and Preliminary Observations on points of Classical interest. Fifth Edition. 8vo. 15s.

——————————— Excerpta ex Ovidii Metam. et Epistolæ. With English Notes, and an Introduction, containing Rules for Construing, a Parsing Praxis, &c. Third Edition. 12mo. 3s. 6d.

——————————— Bellum Catilinarium of Sallust, and Cicero's Four Orations against Catiline; with English Notes and Introduction. Together with the Bellum Jugurthinum of Sallust. Third Edition. 12mo. 3s. 6d.

Truth without Prejudice. Fourth Edition. Small 8vo. 3s. 6d.

Twelve (The) Churches; or, Tracings along the Watling Street. By the Author of "The Red Rose." With Eight Lithographic Plates. Royal 8vo. 3s. 6d.

Vidal's (Mrs.) Tales for the Bush. Originally published in Australia. Fourth Edition. Small 8vo. 5s.

Warter's (Rev. J. W.) The Sea-board and the Down; or, My Parish in the South. In 2 vols. small 4to. Elegantly printed in Antique type, with Illustrations. 28s.

——————————— Plain Practical Sermons. 2 vols. 8vo. 26s.

Warter's (Rev. J. W.) Teaching of the Prayer-book. 8vo. 7s. 6d.

Welchman's Thirty-nine Articles of the Church of England, illustrated with Notes, and confirmed by Texts of Holy Scripture, and Testimonies of the Primitive Fathers; with references to passages in the writings of various Divines. Fifteenth Edition. 8vo. 2s. Or, interleaved with blank paper, 3s.

Wheatly on the Common Prayer; edited by G. E. Corrie, D.D., Master of Jesus College, Examining Chaplain to the Lord Bishop of Ely. 8vo. 10s. 6d.

Wilberforce's (Bp. of Oxford) History of the Protestant Episcopal Church in America. Third Edition. Small 8vo. 5s.

——————————— Rocky Island, and other Similitudes. Twelfth Edition, with Cuts. 18mo. 2s. 6d.

——————————— Sermons preached before the Queen. Sixth Edition, 12mo. 6s.

——————————— Selection of Psalms and Hymns for Public Worship. New Edition. 32mo. 1s. each, or 3l. 10s. per hundred.

Williams's (Rev. Isaac) Devotional Commentary on the Gospel Narrative. 8 vols. small 8vo. 3l. 6s.

Sold separately as follows:—

Thoughts on the Study of the Gospels. 8s.
Harmony of the Evangelists. 8s. 6d.
The Nativity (extending to the Calling of St. Matthew). 8s. 6d.
Second Year of the Ministry. 8s.
Third Year of the Ministry. 8s. 6d.
The Holy Week. 8s. 6d.   The Passion. 8s.
The Resurrection. 8s.

——————————— Apocalypse, with Notes and Reflections. Small 8vo. 8s. 6d.

——————————— Beginning of the Book of Genesis, with Notes and Reflections. Small 8vo. 7s. 6d.

——————————— Sermons on the Characters of the Old Testament. Second Edition. 5s. 6d.

——————————— Female Characters of Holy Scripture; in a Series of Sermons. Second Edition. Small 8vo. 5s. 6d.

——————————— Plain Sermons on the Latter Part of the Catechism; being the Conclusion of the Series contained in the Ninth Volume of "Plain Sermons." 8vo. 6s. 6d.

——————————— Complete Series of Sermons on the Catechism. In one Volume. 13s.

Williams's (Rev. Isaac) Sermons on the Epistle and Gospel for the Sundays and Holy Days throughout the Year. Second Edition. In 3 vols. small 8vo. 16s. 6d.

*** The Third Volume, on the Saints' Days and other Holy Days of the Church, may be had separately, price 5s. 6d.

———————————— **Christian Seasons ; a Series of Poems.** Small 8vo. 3s. 6d.

Wilson's (late Bp. of Sodor and Man) Short and Plain In-struction for the Better Understanding of the Lord's Supper. To which is annexed, The Office of the Holy Communion, with Proper Helps and Directions. Pocket size, 1s. Also, a larger Edition, 2s.

———————————————————— **Sacra Privata; Pri-**vate Meditations and Prayers. Pocket size, 1s. Also, a larger Edition, 2s.

These two Works may be had in various bindings.

Wordsworth's (late Rev. Dr.) Ecclesiastical Biography ; or, Lives of Eminent Men connected with the History of Religion in Eng-land, from the Commencement of the Reformation to the Revolution. Selected, and Illustrated with Notes. Fourth Edition. In 4 vols. 8vo. With 5 Portraits. 2l. 14s.

Wordsworth's (Bp. of St. Andrew's) Christian Boyhood at a Public School : a Collection of Sermons and Lectures delivered at Win-chester College from 1836 to 1846. In 2 vols. 8vo. 1l. 4s.

———————————————— **Catechesis; or, Chris-**tian Instruction preparatory to Confirmation and First Communion. Third Edition. Crown 8vo. 3s. 6d.

Wordsworth's (Canon) New Testament of our Lord and Saviour Jesus Christ, in the original Greek. With Notes, Introductions, and Indexes. New Edition. In Two Vols., imperial 8vo. 4l.

Separately,

Part I.: The Four Gospels. 1l. 1s.
Part II.: The Acts of the Apostles. 10s. 6d.
Part III.: The Epistles of St. Paul. 1l. 11s. 6d.
Part IV.: The General Epistles and Book of Revelation ; with Indexes, 1l. 1s.

———————————————— **Occasional Sermons preached in** Westminster Abbey. In 7 vols. 8vo. Vols. I., II., and III., 7s. each—Vols. IV. and V., 8s. each—Vol. VI., 7s.—Vol. VII., 6s.

———————————— **Theophilus Anglicanus ; or, In-**struction concerning the Principles of the Church Universal and the Church of England. Eighth Edition. 8s. 6d.

———————————————— **Elements of Instruction on the** Church ; being an Abridgment of the above. Second Edition. 2s.

Wordsworth's (Canon) Journal of a Tour in Italy; with
Reflections on the Present Condition and Prospects of Religion in that
Country. 2 vols. post 8vo. 15s.

——————————— On the Inspiration of the Bible.
Five Lectures delivered at Westminster Abbey. 3s. 6d.

——————————— On the Interpretation of the Bible.
Five Lectures delivered at Westminster Abbey. 3s. 6d.

——————— S. Hippolytus and the Church of
Rome in the beginning of the Third Century, from the newly-discovered
" Philosophumena." 8s. 6d.

——————— Letters to M. Gondon, Author of
" Mouvement Religieux en Angleterre," on the Destructive Character of
the Church of Rome, in Religion and Polity. Third Edition. 7s. 6d.

——————————— Sequel to the Above. Second
Edition. 6s. 6d.

——————— On the Canon of Holy Scripture
and on the Apocrypha. Twelve Discourses, preached before the University of Cambridge. With a copious Appendix of Ancient Authorities.
Second Edition. 9s.

——————————— Lectures on the Apocalypse;
preached before the University of Cambridge. Third Edition. 10s. 6d.

——————— Holy Year: Hymns for Sundays
and Holydays, and for other Occasions; with a preface on Hymnology.
Third Edition, in larger type, square 16mo., cloth extra, 4s. 6d. Also
a cheaper Edition, 2s. 6d.

Yonge's (C. D.) History of England from the Earliest
Times to the Peace of Paris, 1856. With a Chronological Table of Contents. In one thick volume, crown 8vo. 12s.

Though available as a School-book, this volume contains as much as
three ordinary octavos. It is written on a carefully digested plan, ample
space being given to the last three centuries. All the best authorities have
been consulted.

Arnold's Practical Introductions to Greek, Latin, &c.

Henry's First Latin Book. Sixteenth Edition. 12mo. 3s.

The value of this popular School-book is sufficiently shown by its very general use, not only throughout England, but in America and many of our Colonies. About 180,000 copies have already been sold, and the sale is still increasing.

A Second Latin Book, and Practical Grammar. Intended as a Sequel to Henry's First Latin Book. Seventh Edition. 12mo. 4s.

A First Verse Book, Part I.; intended as an easy Introduction to the Latin Hexameter and Pentameter. Seventh Edition. 12mo. 2s.

A First Verse Book, Part II.; containing additional Exercises. Second Edition. 1s.

Historiæ Antiquæ Epitome, from *Cornelius Nepos, Justin,* &c. With English Notes, Rules for Construing, Questions, Geographical Lists, &c. Seventh Edition. 4s.

A First Classical Atlas, containing fifteen Maps, coloured in outline; intended as a Companion to the *Historiæ Antiquæ Epitome.* 8vo. 7s. 6d.

A Practical Introduction to Latin Prose Composition. Part I. Eleventh Edition. 8vo. 6s. 6d.

This Work is founded on the principles of imitation and frequent repetition. It is at once a Syntax, a Vocabulary, and an Exercise Book; and considerable attention has been paid to the subject of Synonymes. It is now used at all, or nearly all, the public schools.

A Practical Introduction to Latin Prose Composition, Part II.; containing the Doctrine of Latin Particles, with Vocabulary, an Antibarbarus, &c. Fourth Edition. 8vo. 8s.

A Practical Introduction to Latin Verse Composition. 8vo. Third Edition. 5s. 6d.

Contents:—1. "Ideas" for Hexameter and Elegiac Verses. 2. Alcaics. 3. Sapphics. 4. The other Horatian Metres. 5. Appendix of Poetical Phraseology, and Hints on Versification.

Gradus ad Parnassum Novus Anticlepticus; founded on
Quicherat's *Thesaurus Poeticus Linguæ Latinæ.* 8vo. *half-bound.* 10s. 6d.

*** A Prospectus, with specimen page, may be had of the Publishers.

Longer Latin Exercises; Part I. Third Edition. 8vo. 4s.

The object of this Work is to supply boys with an easy collection of *short* passages, as an Exercise Book for those who have gone once, at least, through the First Part of the Editor's " Practical Introduction to Latin Prose Composition."

Longer Latin Exercises, Part II.; containing a Selection of Passages of greater length, in genuine idiomatic English, for Translation into Latin. 8vo. 4s.

Materials for Translation into Latin: selected and arranged by Augustus Grotefend. Translated from the German by the Rev. H. H. Arnold, B.A., with Notes and Excursuses. Third Edition. 8vo. 7s. 6d.

A Copious and Critical English-Latin Lexicon, by the Rev. T. K. Arnold and the Rev. J. E. Riddle. Sixth Edition. 1l. 5s.

An Abridgment of the above Work, for the Use of Schools. By the Rev. J. C. Ebden, late Fellow and Tutor of Trinity Hall, Cambridge. Square 12mo. *bound.* 10s. 6d.

The First Greek Book; on the Plan of "Henry's First Latin Book." Fourth Edition. 12mo. 5s.

The Second Greek Book (on the same Plan); containing an Elementary Treatise on the Greek Particles and the Formation of Greek Derivatives. 12mo. 5s. 6d.

A Practical Introduction to Greek Accidence. With Easy Exercises and Vocabulary. Seventh Edition. 8vo. 5s. 6d.

A Practical Introduction to Greek Prose Composition, Part I. Ninth Edition. 8vo. 5s. 6d.

*** The object of this Work is to enable the Student, as soon as he can decline and conjugate with tolerable facility, to translate simple sentences after given examples, and with given words; the principles trusted to being principally those of *imitation and very frequent repetition.* It is at once a Syntax, a Vocabulary, and an Exercise Book.

A Greek Grammar; intended as a sufficient Grammar of reference for Schools and Colleges. Second Edition. 8vo. *half-bound.* 10s. 6d.

Professor Madvig's Syntax of the Greek Language, especially
of the Attic Dialect; translated by the Rev. Henry Browne, M.A.
Together with an Appendix on the Greek Particles; by the Translator.
Square 8vo. 8s. 6d.

An Elementary Greek Grammar. 12mo. 5s.; or, with
Dialects, 6s.

Some Account of the Greek Dialects, for the Use of Beginners; being an Appendix to "An Elementary Greek Grammar."
12mo. 1s. 6d.

A Complete Greek and English Lexicon for the Poems of
Homer, and the Homeridæ. Translated from the German of Crusius,
by Professor Smith. New and Revised Edition. 9s. half-bound.

₊ A Prospectus and specimen of this Lexicon may be had.

A Copious Phraseological English-Greek Lexicon, founded
on a work prepared by J. W. Frädersdorff, Ph. Dr. of the Taylor-Institu-
tion, Oxford. Revised, Enlarged, and Improved by the Rev. T. K. Arnold,
M.A., formerly Fellow of Trinity College, Cambridge, and Henry Browne,
M.A., Vicar of Pevensey, and Prebendary of Chichester. Third Edition,
corrected, with the Appendix incorporated. 8vo. 21s.

₊ A Prospectus, with specimen page, may be had.

Classical Examination Papers. A Series of 93 Extracts
from Greek, Roman, and English Classics for Translation, with occasional
Questions and Notes; each extract on a separate leaf. Price of the whole
in a specimen packet, 4s., or six copies of any Separate Paper may be had
for 3d.

Keys to the following may be had by Tutors only:

First Latin Book, 1s.   Second Latin Book, 2s.
                    Cornelius Nepos, 1s.
First Verse Book, 1s.   Latin Verse Composition, 2s.
        Latin Prose Composition, Parts I. and II., 1s. 6d. each.
Longer Latin Exercises, Part I., 1s. 6d.   Part II., 2s. 6d.
    Greek Prose Composition, Part I., 1s. 6d.   Part II., 4s. 6d.
            First Greek Book, 1s. 6d.   Second, 2s.

The First Hebrew Book; on the Plan of "Henry's First
Latin Book." 12mo. Second Edition. 7s. 6d.   The Key, 3s. 6d.

The Second Hebrew Book, containing the Book of Genesis;
together with a Hebrew Syntax, and a Vocabulary and Grammatical
Commentary. 9s.

The First German Book; on the Plan of "Henry's First Latin Book." By the Rev. T. K. Arnold and Dr. Frädersdorff. Fifth Edition. 12mo. 5s. 6d. The Key, 2s. 6d.

A Reading Companion to the First German Book; containing Extracts from the best Authors, with a Vocabulary and Notes. 12mo. Second Edition. 4s.

The Second German Book; a Syntax, and Etymological Vocabulary, with copious Reading-Lessons and Exercises. Edited by Dr. Frädersdorff. 6s. 6d. Key to the English Exercises, 1s.

_____

The First French Book; on the Plan of "Henry's First Latin Book." Fifth Edition. 12mo. 5s. 6d. Key to the Exercises, by Delille, 2s. 6d.

_____

Henry's English Grammar; a Manual for Beginners. 12mo. 3s. 6d.

Spelling turned Etymology. Second Edition. 12mo. 2s. 6d.

The Pupil's Book, (a Companion to the above,) 1s. 3d.

Latin viâ English; being the Second Part of the above Work. 12mo. 4s. 6d.

An English Grammar for Classical Schools; being a Practical Introduction to "English Prose Composition." Sixth Edition. 12mo. 4s. 6d.

_____

Arnold's Handbooks for the Classical Student, with Questions.

Ancient History and Geography. Translated from the German of Pütz, by the Ven. Archdeacon Paul. Second Edition. 12mo. 6s. 6d.

Mediæval History and Geography. Translated from the German of Pütz. By the same. 12mo. 4s. 6d.

Modern History and Geography. Translated from the German of Pütz. By the same. 12mo. 5s. 6d.

Grecian Antiquities. By Professor Bojesen. Translated from the German Version of Dr. Hoffa. By the same. Second Edition. 12mo. 3s. 6d.

Roman Antiquities. · By Professor Bojesen. Second Edition.
3s. 6d.

Hebrew Antiquities. By the Rev. Henry Browne, M.A.
Prebendary of Chichester. 12mo. 4s.

₊ This Work describes the manners and customs of the ancient
Hebrews which were common to them with other nations, and the rites
and ordinances which distinguished them as the chosen people Israel.

Greek Synonymes. From the French of Pillon. 6s. 6d.

Latin Synonymes. From the German of Döderlein. Translated by the Rev. H. H. Arnold. Second Edition. 4s.

Arnold's School Classics.

Cornelius Nepos, Part I.; with Critical Questions and An-
swers, and an imitative Exercise on each Chapter. Fourth Edition.
12mo. 4s.

Eclogæ Ovidianæ, with English Notes; Part I. (from the
Elegiac Poems.) Tenth Edition. 12mo. 2s. 6d.

Eclogæ Ovidianæ, Part II. (from the Metamorphoses.) 5s.

The Æneid of Virgil, with English Notes from Dübner.
12mo. 6s.

Eclogæ Horatianæ; Carmina prope Omnia continens. Ad-
dita est Familiaris Interpretatio ex Adnotationibus Mitscherlichii,
Doeringii, Orellii, aliorum excerpta. Second Edition. 12mo. 5s.

₊ All the objectionable passages are omitted from this Edition.

The Works of Horace, followed by English Introductions
and Notes, abridged and adapted for School use, from the Edition of
Fr. Dübner. In one volume, 12mo. 7s.

Cicero.—Selections from his Orations, with English Notes,
from the best and most recent sources. Contents:—The Fourth Book of
the Impeachment of Verres, the Four Speeches against Catiline, and the
Speech for the Poet Archias. 12mo. Second Edition. 4s.

Cicero, Part II.; containing Selections from his Epistles,
arranged in the order of time, with Accounts of the Consuls, Events of
each year, &c. With English Notes from the best Commentators, especially Matthiæ. 12mo. 5s.

Cicero, Part III.; containing the Tusculan Disputations
(entire). With English Notes from Tischer, by the Rev. Archdeacon
Paul. 5s. 6d.

Cicero, Part IV.; containing De Finibus Malorum et Bo-
norum. (On the Supreme Good.) With a Preface, English Notes, &c.,
partly from Madvig and others, by the Rev. James Beaven, D.D., late
Professor of Theology in King's College, Toronto. 12mo. 5s. 6d.

Cicero, Part V.; containing Cato Major, sive De Senectute
Dialogus; with English Notes from Sommerbrodt, by the Rev. Henry
Browne, M.A., Canon of Chichester. 12mo. 2s. 6d.

Homer for Beginners.—The First Three Books of the Iliad,
with English Notes; forming a sufficient Commentary for Young Students.
Second Edition. 12mo. 3s. 6d.

Homer. — The Iliad Complete, with English Notes and
Grammatical References. Second Edition. In one thick volume, 12mo.
half-bound. 12s.

In this Edition, the Argument of each Book is divided into short Sections, which are prefixed to those portions of the Text, respectively, which
they describe. The Notes (principally from Dübner) are at the foot of
each page. At the end of the volume are useful Appendices.

Homer.—The Iliad, Books I. to IV.; with a Critical Introduction, and copious English Notes. Second Edition. 12mo. 7s. 6d.

Demosthenes, with English Notes from the best and most
recent sources, Sauppe, Doberenz, Jacobs, Dissen, Westermann, &c.

The Olynthiac Orations. Second Edition. 12mo. 3s.
The Oration on the Crown. Second Edition. 12mo. 4s. 6d.
The Philippic Orations. Second Edition. 12mo. 4s.

Æschines.—Speech against Ctesiphon. 12mo. 4s.

The Text is that of Baiter and Sauppe; the Notes are by Professor
Champlin, with additional Notes by President Woolsey and the Editor.

Sophocles, with English Notes, from Schneidewin. By the
Rev. Archdeacon Paul, and the Rev. Henry Bowne, M.A.

The Ajax. 3s.—The Philoctetes. 3s.—The Œdipus Tyrannus. 4s.—
The Œdipus Coloneus. 4s.—The Antigone. 4s.

Euripides, with English Notes, from Hartung, Dübner,
Witzschel, Schöne, &c.

The Hecuba.—The Hippolytus.—The Bacchæ.—The Medea.—The
Iphigenia in Tauris, 3s. each.

Aristophanes.—Eclogæ Aristophanicæ, with English Notes,
by Professor Felton. Part I. (The Clouds.) 12mo. 3s. 6d. Part II.
(The Birds.) 3s. 6d.

⁎ In this Edition the objectionable passages are omitted.

Lightning Source UK Ltd.
Milton Keynes UK
UKHW022151250919
350449UK00008B/146/P